The Belief in Wings

Donloyn LeDuff Gadson

Creole Magnolia Publishing

2016 Creole Magnolia Publishing Trade Paperback Edition

Copyright © 2016 Donloyn LeDuff Gadson

ISBN: 0-9982952-0-5
ISBN-13: 978-0-9982952-0-6

For my daughters Lauryn, Kourtney and Chloe.

And for the young girl I once was and dreamed to be.

"Therefore, if anyone is in Christ, he is a new creation; old things have passed away; behold, all things have become new."

2 Corinthians 5:17, NKJV

CONTENTS

STAGE I – VOICE: THE CATERPILLAR

STAGE II – COURAGE: THE CHRYSALIS

ACKNOWLEDGMENTS

This project has been a labor of love. So much has gone into its creation. So many wonderful people have contributed to its release. I'd like to thank them all here.

First, all thanks, praise, honor and glory must go to Our Almighty Father, Jehovah God. Thank you Father for Your Son, Jesus Christ; Your Holy Spirit; Your Word, guidance, mercy, favor and grace. Father, words cannot express my gratitude. I am humbled by your awesome power.

To my husband, Aastan. Thank you for your love and support. Thank you for believing in me and talking me off the ledge when the going got tough. Thank you for picking up the slack when I needed extra time to work. And thank you for the late nights you sat up finalizing book cover images. You know better than anyone all that has gone into this book. Thanks for being there.

My precious daughter Lauryn...you inspire me. You always have. Your smile, your sweetness and your goofy ways. And let's not forget your British accents and impressions! You've been a constant reminder of why I decided to write this book, who it's for and how it will help. Thank you for agreeing to be on its cover.

Many thanks to Dana Klein of Photography by Dana for creating an exquisite storybook image for the cover. Your insight and talents captured the dreamy wonder that is the heart of this book. When I look at this book's cover, I believe!

My deepest love and gratitude to my editor, Cindi Carver-Futch. Cindi, thank you not only for editing this book, but also for loving me through it. You are my mentor, my sister and my friend. Your wisdom has been the greatest gift. You encourage me to dig deeper, to explore further and fly higher. You've been a rich blessing in my life, and I could not have done this without you.

To my other daughters, Kourtney and Chloe…thank you for always reminding me what it means to look at the world with excitement and hope. To my five amazing sons, Brandon, Noah, John-Paul, Allen-Michael and Thomas…thank you all for being awesome young men. I am so proud of each of you.

To my mother-in-law, Alma and my incredible friends…I love you all. Thank you for your prayers, love and support. You've encouraged me, laughed with me, cried with me, shared scriptures and prayed me through some rough moments. I am blessed, humbled and filled with gratitude.

To Lori…you've believed in my wings from the beginning. Thank you for finding me. Thank you for loving me unconditionally. Thank you for holding my hand through my hero's journey and being that safe place to fall. Even after being separated all those years, the love always remained.

And finally, to my mom and dad…I know the mere mention of my ordeal is hard for you. It was a difficult time for us all. Thank you for respecting the way I've chosen to help others through my story. Thank you for allowing me the space and freedom to heal on my own terms. Thank you for your prayers, support and love. I hope I've made you both proud to call me yours.

DONLOYN LEDUFF GADSON

Dear young lady holding these pages,

Because of my story, I have written this book for you. We're going to take a journey…a three-part, transformational passage through voice, courage and power. This journey is modeled after the last three stages of a butterfly. As we move through each stage, I will share principles, poetry and opportunities for personal reflection. I will also share some of my own personal journey — parts of my narrative that I know will help you. I understand how difficult this process can be. My evolution was far more arduous than necessary. Yours doesn't have to be that way. I am here to make sure it is not. As you embark upon this adventure, I promise to help you move from that place of self-doubt to one of personal power.

Before we begin, I want you to know a few things. You are a butterfly. I know you may not feel or look like one right now. But at the end of this book, you will. I understand you are filled with doubt. But you are remarkable and gifted in more ways than you can comprehend. It is my mission to help you realize that. You have wings designed for greatness. That greatness, once activated, becomes a light. A brilliant, blinding light that is ready to shine out upon the world. It is a light that wants to burst forth and illuminate all in its path, even the darkened, forgotten spaces. It is your sole purpose to allow it to do so. Through the sharing of your unique talents and with the spreading of your powerful wings, you are to allow your light to shine for all to see. In doing so, you honor God and bring fulfillment to yourself, all while blessing the lives of others.

I cannot lie to you. There will be hard times. There likely have been already. Repeated attacks designed to silence you, kill your spirit and diminish your value will happen. You cannot allow those painful experiences to frighten you and stop you from feeding your identity. Your identity is your voice. Right now, as you begin this journey, you are a precious caterpillar. And just as the caterpillar feeds itself continuously, your voice must also be nourished. The good news is that the evil of this world is no match for your hunger to flourish. Continue to feast on inspiration, and you will thrive. Continue to grow in your identity, and you will never doubt your voice. You will be confident in who you are.

There will be times when you feel alone, afraid and unsure. Times when your innocence seems too weak to sustain the difficulty of change. Times when transformation feels like a battlefield. Fear will challenge you. Ah, but what a courageous one you are! You may not know this now, but you are valiant. You will step into your chrysalis unafraid and, as the commander of your own destiny, you will be victorious. As you move through tests and trials, be strong and stand tall in your faith. Be brave. Choose courage. Emerge with the wings of a butterfly, Young Warrior, for YOU are the hero of your story.

The power within you is immense. It is intimidating for some. Those are the ones who will try to control it...to ravish your freedom, contain it and keep it for themselves. They believe stealing your power fuels their own. They will confuse you and leave you feeling incapable and without purpose. But because the source of your power is bigger than you, it knows neither limits nor boundaries. It can never be consumed, contained or destroyed. It has always been right there. It was designed specifically for you. It rests upon your wings. You must simply open them, My Butterfly, and believe.

Believe in your wings.

Let's get started!

Donlayn

DONLOYN LEDUFF GADSON

<u>BEFORE WE BEGIN</u>

The Belief in Wings...just writing those words takes me to a place—a starry, dreamy place filled with hope, greatness and every possibility my heart and imagination have crafted.

We all have wings - our personal power, our inherent ability to soar after our dreams...accomplishing great things...making a difference in the world. It is mind-blowing the number of people who don't believe in their wings. But even I didn't always believe in mine.

When we are children, we are taught to believe in fantasy. Santa Claus. The Tooth Fairy. The Easter Bunny. We are encouraged to look upon those sweet childhood myths with a dreamy-eyed gaze of excitement. Children are told to believe wholeheartedly in their power and reality. Now, none of these things actually exist. Neither does the potential for them. Yet, year after year, children are asked to believe in the power of these magical figures.

Why aren't more of us as children asked to believe in the very real and magical possibilities that exist within ourselves? Wouldn't it be better if we were constantly encouraged to have these same thoughts and ideas regarding our own power?

Unfortunately, too few of us receive reminders about the dreams and greatness that can be realized if we believe in ourselves. We aren't reminded that our inherent power requires our belief. We aren't told to believe in our wings even though we don't see them yet.

We aren't even told we have wings.

Why is that?

Doubt is the culprit. Doubt is a powerful infection—a destructive epidemic easily spread to others. It's cyclical. And unless that cycle is broken, it will be passed on.

For years, I was consumed with self-doubt. I didn't believe in the existence of a great power residing within me waiting to be released. I didn't believe in this great power's ability to transform me.

And I certainly didn't believe that my growth was a metamorphosis that would result in powerful wings taking shape and lifting me to all the places I had ever dared to dream.

Metaphorically speaking, we are butterflies. And like the butterfly, we must evolve through stages. Each of these stages requires we master the step prior. Before you can be a butterfly, you must spend time perfecting your growth in the chrysalis. And before you can enter the chrysalis, you must fulfill your caterpillar experience.

When a caterpillar is born, its mission is to eat as much as it possibly can, to take in as much nourishment as it can find. It roams about freely, consuming all the leafy goodness in its environment. If this development remains undisturbed, then this stage will progress properly. And before long, a healthy caterpillar will be ready to enter its chrysalis.

However, if there are bees or wasps buzzing around, this becomes a problem for the caterpillar. It is rational for caterpillars to fear the buzzing of wasps. Wasps will eat caterpillars and represent a real danger. Bees are not harmful, but they buzz like wasps. Since caterpillars cannot differentiate between the buzzing of bees and the buzzing of wasps, they are afraid of them both. Filled with fear and doubt, they abandon their mission of eating and hurry to a safe place. As a result, the growth and nourishment of the caterpillar is interrupted. If this happens often enough, the caterpillar will not progress through the chrysalis stage to discover its wings.

Right now, you are that caterpillar. And the hustle and bustle and problems and craziness that exist in this world create fears – rational and irrational - that whir and buzz about filling you with doubt and distracting you from your main job of nourishing yourself.

That buzzing…that noise…it is the birthplace of self-doubt. And just as it affects the caterpillar, that noise paralyzes you, regardless of its source. Be it from internal thoughts or outside sources… from rational or irrational fears…the self-doubt that results can interrupt your growth and prevent you from developing your individuality. Whether the noise is trying to drown you out, silence you or ignore you, its goal is to make you feel insignificant and worthless by any means necessary.

I was a doubtful caterpillar. My life was filled with so much noise — noise generated from painful experiences and learned fears. Not only that, but nourishing words like Dream, Inspiration, Belief, Hope, Determination, Clarity, Voice, Courage, Passion, Purpose, Bravery, Creativity and Possibility were not part of the vernacular spoken in my household growing up. I didn't even notice these concepts until I was in my twenties. They were foreign to me.

But when I did notice them, I thought they were beautiful. I began to pick them up. I added them to my proverbial picnic basket of wisdom, and feasted on them along my way. I allowed these concepts to be my "leaves," to nourish me, to nourish my identity, to nourish my belief in possibilities.

If you are in this place of self-doubt and don't believe there is any shred of power within you, it's not too late. You can do the same. You must recognize the "leaves" when you see them, and feast on them. Do not allow the buzzing to fill you with irrational fear and doubt. Do not allow the noise to drown out your child-like sense of wonder. Keep that hopeful, starry-eyed gaze when you dream of all the things you can accomplish.

There is great power that exists within you, but you must keep nourishing yourself. You must keep feeding your belief in wings…long before you ever see them. And before you know it, you will not only see them, you will feel them… lifting you up with power to fly high and achieve your dreams.

What do the following words mean to you? Do any of them have a special meaning in your life right now?

Dream:_____

_____

_____

Inspiration:_____

_____

_____

Belief:_____

_____

_____

Hope:_____

_____

_____

Determination:_____

_____

_____

Clarity:_____

_____

_____

Voice:_____

_____

_____

Courage:_____

_____

_____

Passion:_____

_____

_____

Purpose:_____

_____

_____

Bravery:_____

_____

_____

Creativity:_____

_____

_____

Possibility:_____

_____

_____

STAGE I

VOICE

THE CATERPILLAR

DONLOYN LEDUFF GADSON

CHAPTER 1

<u>THE NEED TO BE HEARD</u>

Every person has a deep need to be heard…a persistent need to feel someone is listening. People need to be heard because we all want to know we are important. We want to know we are loved. We all need to feel that we matter to another person, that we're not in this alone. When another person hears you, sees you and takes the time to listen to you, that is a display of love. And we were created to love and to receive love.

Because of the imperfections that exist in this world, displays of love oftentimes fall flat. Our voices aren't always heard. Remember, the craziness of life creates a whirring sound, a noise that becomes the birthplace of doubt. This doubt drowns out and overpowers the love. Thus, drowning out your voice. Most of us understand what it feels like to be drowned out by the noise…to have our voices go unheard. The noise can become so loud it's frightening. Just as the caterpillar hurries to safety, we withdraw also. It silences us. It disrupts our growth, and we become lost. When the direction of your life is interrupted, you become filled with uncertainty, and your journey becomes almost impossible to navigate.

My first memory of trying to be heard takes me back to Vallejo, California in 1978, in a small house on Loyola Way. It was a school day. I was five-years-old. Each morning, my dad would wake me by gently stroking my face with a warm washcloth as he recited the following words:

> "Good Morning birds
> Good morning bees
> Good morning weeping willow trees
> Good morning stars
> Good morning sun
> Good morning everyone"

And each morning, my father would take me to the babysitter's house where I would eat breakfast and then walk myself to school. When the school day was done, I would walk back to the babysitter's house and wait for my father to pick up my baby brother and me.

But on this particular morning, I began crying to my dad. I told him I didn't want to go to the babysitter's house that day. I tried to get the words out the best way I knew how, but I was unable to articulate my feelings. My tears were placeholders, filling in the gaps where words needed to be. Despite my child-like attempts, all my dad was able to hear was a cranky child carrying on, interrupting the morning routine. I can still see us standing in the doorway of my bedroom. I got in trouble that morning.

What he didn't hear, what I tried so desperately to say in my little girl voice, was that I was being molested, sexually abused by my babysitter's fifteen-year-old son. I was trying to tell him what was happening to me in that house. That I was not safe there. That I was afraid. I needed to be protected. But, before I could be protected, I needed to be heard.

My babysitter was a lady in the neighborhood who operated an in-home daycare. Her house was close to ours and only two streets away from my school. Mrs. Smith was her name. I remember her being a mean lady. I was so afraid of her. Petrified. Although she was friendly when my parents were around, she didn't seem to care for me at all. For what reason, I'll never know.

She had three sons. And, it wasn't long before her middle son, D___ Smith, set his sights on me. His mother allowed him to take me to his room, away from the other children she watched. He even used my fear of her against me. He would threaten to tell his mother that I had broken the rules if I didn't cooperate with his demands. For months, I endured this constant torture.

I often wondered if D___ Smith's mother knew what inappropriate things he was doing to me. His older brother knew what was happening. He even had the opportunity to rescue me once. It was a very small house, and D___ Smith would take me into his bedroom and close the door. One day, his older brother found us there. I looked at him…right in his eyes. My expression must have been pleading for help, because he looked at D___ Smith and said, "Man, why don't you just leave her alone." D___ Smith responded by mumbling a few insignificant words and shooed his brother away. I was left there alone with him…trapped behind closed doors. And again, my voice went unheard.

This ongoing molestation and mental anguish is what caused me to cry out to my father on that morning…that morning when I couldn't find the words. That morning when I could only muster tears. That morning I was seen as disruptive. That morning I was not heard.

Months passed by and eventually my parents learned of my abuse. But it took years, decades, for me to overcome the heartache that came with crying out to my daddy for help but receiving punishment instead. I always knew it wasn't my dad's fault; he didn't know. And I certainly didn't know how to tell him. But, it still hurt.

After the horror unfolded in Vallejo, my parents sold our home, and we moved to the east coast. My family and I fled from the darkness of California and settled into our new life in South Carolina. Aside from a brief stint with a child psychiatrist, my abuse was never discussed. My parents wanted to protect me from the pain. To spare us all the torment of rehashing such painful memories. So they kept silent. Unbeknownst to them, that silence would prove to be detrimental to my voice.

Another memory of not being heard occurred when I was approximately 10 years old. My mother's professional position put her in the unique spot of rubbing elbows with citizens in the heart of the city. From attorneys, doctors and politicians to the retired elderly, college students and homeless folks living on the streets, my mother came to know the locals quite well.

One Friday evening, we pulled into the parking lot of a fast food restaurant downtown near my mom's office. Mama didn't cook on Fridays. That's how I clearly remember what day of the week it was. It was a break for her and a treat for us kids. We went into the restaurant to place our order when suddenly a young man with Down's syndrome grabbed me. Before I could I understand what was happening, I was in his arms. He began groping me. Squeezing me tightly, he kept trying to kiss me and repeatedly professed his love for me. I can still hear his words today. Horrified, I struggled to free myself. I cried out to my mother to make him stop. "Mama! Mama!"

My mother knew this young man. He was a part of the community with which she had become so familiar and comfortable. She knew he had a disability. She also knew he didn't mean me any harm. She knew he demonstrated this display of affection to many people on a regular basis. In her adult mind, I was to grant him a free pass for his behavior just as every other adult in the community had grown accustomed to doing. Although he was a young adult, he didn't understand that what he was doing was making me uncomfortable. However, I was expected to understand. But my ten-year-old self didn't care about his limitations. What my mother didn't realize was that as a ten-year-old survivor of rape and sexual abuse, he *was* harming me. While she was trying to teach me to be accepting and understanding of those with limitations and differences, I was having flashbacks of being violated. My mother meant well, but I needed it to stop. That day, I lifted my voice. I cried out for help, but received none. And again, I was not heard.

This pattern of not being heard became a constant in my life. No matter how I chose to express my voice, I was shut down. I loved to sing, but I was repeatedly quieted and unfairly compared to others. I discovered my love and gift for drawing. I was a good artist with a great deal of potential. All I needed was encouragement and continued practice. But again, I was met with the same disapproval. No matter how I attempted to share my voice, I was silenced. I went unnoticed and unheard.

I realize these stories may seem intense. But I share them for one reason only...to illustrate that feeling as though no one hears you is a lonely place to be. It's a torture chamber of isolation where all you hear is your own voice bouncing off the walls, "Am I invisible? Why doesn't anyone hear me?"

I could share dozens of situations with you that resulted in my being unheard. From the time I was a little girl up through my teenage years and well into my twenties, I felt alone, isolated and uncertain. No one understood all I had been through...all I was going through. I didn't understand it myself. It got to the point where I could barely hear the sound of my own voice.

If you're holding these pages, then I'm certain you've felt this way at some point in your life. Your story may not involve abuse—I pray that it doesn't—but no matter what circumstances your narrative holds, we all understand the fundamental need to be heard.

The need to be heard is a hunger. And much like it drives the caterpillar, that hunger is what drives you to explore and learn. As you explore and learn, you grow. And as you grow, the more you begin to dream, inspire, believe, hope and create. Your passion, purpose and determination come alive. You develop the belief that makes all things seem possible. When you feed that hunger, your voice—your identity—becomes clear and certain.

What's your first memory of sharing your voice?

_____

_____

_____

_____

_____

_____

_____

_____

Reflect on a time when you felt your voice went unheard or was drowned out by the noise.

_____

_____

_____

_____

_____

_____

_____

_____

How do you feel about the need to be heard? Use the space below to express your thoughts in any style you choose. Use a poem, a journal entry, a drawing, photos or brainstorm. Be creative!

_____

_____

_____

_____

_____

_____

_____

_____

_____

_____

_____

_____

_____

_____

_____

_____

_____

_____

i just need to be heard

you there, sir

can you lend me your ear?

i'm sharing wonderful things

i know you'd love to hear

you there, ma'am

can you hear me now?

i opened my heart

did it not make a sound?

you there, friend

my heart has been broken

but it will surely mend

if your advice is spoken

you there, mom

why can't you understand?

i just need you to listen

please take my hand

you there, daddy
your little girl's in need
i need you to hear me
please, take heed

you there…anyone
can you not feel my words?
i feel so unloved
i just need to be heard

DONLOYN LEDUFF GADSON

CHAPTER 2

<u>LONGING TO BELONG</u>

In addition to needing to be heard, we all want to feel a sense of belonging. We want to know that we are not just being tolerated, but accepted…completely accepted and included for all we are. We want to know that we belong. That we have a place among everyone else.

The common pitfall here is that we convince ourselves that in order to "fit in," we must change who we are and adopt the characteristics, ideas, looks and mannerisms of others. But sometimes the very ones with whom you are longing to fit in expect you to do just that. Or they shun you for not being like they are…not thinking as they think. I struggled with this issue for many years. And it hurt. Effective, authentic voice doesn't want to be bullied into changing, nor does it want to barge its way in. It wants to be invited…welcomed with love, respect and appreciation. Even when what it has to say differs from that of all other voices in the room. If this is where you are or if this is where you have been, please know that you are not alone.

I am multiracial. You may know many people who define themselves this way. Or you yourself may come from a diverse lineage. It may not seem like a big deal. However, in the time and place in which I grew up, it was a big deal. I didn't belong. I was viewed as an outsider. I wasn't White enough. I wasn't Black enough. I wasn't this or that enough. I wasn't any one thing enough for people to feel comfortable with my identity. They didn't know what "box" I belonged in, and that bothered them.

People will try to assign you meaning. They will try to force upon you the voice and identity they feel you should display. And based on that, they will try to decide where you belong and where you fit in, if at all.

Desperate attempts to place me in their boxes of conformity and assimilation always opened the door for questions like, "What are you?" or "What are you mixed with?" or "Why is your hair like that?" My peers would isolate me by saying things like, "You're not Black!" or "*We* don't consider *you* Black." And between you and me, that last one hurt a lot.

Because the word *we* drove home the point that multiple groups of people felt this way about me. That there was this collective voice to which I was not allowed to contribute—a collective voice that didn't want any part of me.

I was called names. Wannabe… White girl… Mutt…
Heinz 57… House "N-word"…"N-word"… Red… Yellow…
just to name a few. I was even told that I was a product of
rape, that slave masters had raped my ancestors and that's
how I came to be. Can you imagine how ashamed and
ostracized I felt after hearing that? There I was, a sexual
abuse and rape victim (because at that time I felt like a
victim and not a survivor), being told that I am also the
result of abuse and rape! Was this all I would ever be, a
victim of abuse? Was this all the future had for me? That
solidified my misguided notion that I had to keep my
molestation and rape a secret, because they would surely
hate me if they found out. Or, at least, that's what I thought.

In addition to having a diverse heritage, I struggled with
the concept of home. My family and I moved around a lot in
my younger years, so I felt had no place to call my own. My
family was from Louisiana, but I was born in Florida. By the
time I was six, we had lived in Florida, South Carolina,
Massachusetts, California, and then back to Charleston, SC.
I felt I was from nowhere and everywhere. I felt displaced. I
was viewed as an outsider, and I felt like one.

When I was younger, it was very common to hear native
Charleston families refer to their fellow Charleston area

residents as "Come Ya" or "Been Ya." *Come Ya* means you and your family came to Charleston from somewhere else. *Been Ya* means your family has always been here…you're a native. My family and I were considered Come Ya, and unfortunately, there were countless times we were treated as such. All I wanted was to be a part of something. To belong. I wanted to feel embraced, not pushed away. I wanted to feel wanted. But who would want the little light-skinned girl who had no home and the scars of rape? In my mind, the answer to that question was no one.

Let me tell you something about the "Need to be Heard" and "Longing to Belong." Sometimes, they contradict one another. They don't always co-exist. It is possible, but it doesn't always happen. Here's why… In a perfect world, we would all have the freedom to express our uniquely created selves while simultaneously experiencing acceptance and love despite our differences. Newsflash! This is not a perfect world. And although you may long to have others completely embrace you, you must face the harsh reality that some people will reject you for simply being different…for simply being YOU.

You see, when you honor the need to be heard, it means you have made the bold decision to stand out, to add your unique, bright twinkle to a night filled with stars. When you cling to that need to have your voice acknowledged, there will never be a box that could possibly contain all the gifts you bring. Your beauty, your talents and your abilities will rise to the brim and spill over its edges.

Although we have a natural and healthy need to belong, that need oftentimes translates into conforming or "fitting in." Belonging and fitting in are two different things. Longing to belong to something is normal. But if you feel like you can't find where you belong and you're desperate to find a place to fit in, you'll do almost anything. This can result in compromising your beliefs and standards. When we conform to the views, opinions and expectations of others, we abandon who we are. We abandon our character and our voices begin to blend in and eventually fade away. That outcome is in direct opposition to having our voices heard.

Does that mean we should abandon the desire to belong? Of course not. Just because the world repeatedly sends the same flawed message that fitting in means squelching our individuality and following the crowd, it doesn't mean we have to consent to that. It is possible to embrace your singularity and all that makes you unique while at the same time feeling a sense of belonging and acceptance from others. But what you must realize and accept is that you will not be received with open arms by everyone. And that is absolutely okay.

When you find yourself wrestling with these two desires, it is vital that you choose the need to be heard. The need to be heard requires boldness…courage…the grit necessary to embrace vulnerability and share your true self. Yielding to the longing to belong can easily lead to the trap of fitting in. Fitting in requires none of the aforementioned strengths. Cowardice. Groupthink. Assimilation. Those are the only prerequisites.

If we confuse the longing to belong with the desire to fit in, we could end up succumbing to the buzzing…hurrying to a safe place to escape the noise. The desire to fit in opens the door for the fear of rejection. This fear will distract you from nourishing your identity. Remember, in this first stage, you are the caterpillar. Don't let the fear of the bees and the wasps keep you from feasting on the leaves; your voice must be fed.

Although the need to be heard and the longing to belong don't always peacefully co-exist, it doesn't mean they cannot. So the question becomes, "How can I honor my need

to be heard while garnering a deep sense of belonging?"
Here's the answer:

As you give way to the need to be heard, you cultivate
your identity. Your voice will become loud and booming.
Not obnoxious and overpowering. But grand and strong.
Your voice will become like a mighty trumpet sounding out
from the highest mountaintop, calling all those who value
not only *your* voice, but also the unique identities of others.
These will be the people to whom you belong. And as others
begin to gravitate toward you, make it a part of your mission
to provide a place of belonging for them. As you nourish,
develop and raise your voice, become that person who
makes others feel accepted and valued, regardless of their
differences.

No one wants to feel pushed away or ousted from the
group. I know you've felt that way at some point. I know it
feels lonely. It's like being alone on a tiny, deserted island.
But keep developing your voice. The right ones will hear
you. And when they do, that tiny island won't feel so lonely
and deserted. You just might discover it is a beautiful island
resort fill with wonderful people just like you!

Write about a time when you felt rejected or like you didn't belong. Did you try to fit in, or did you remain true to your identity?

_____

_____

_____

_____

_____

_____

_____

_____

_____

_____

_____

_____

_____

_____

_____

If you remain true to your need to be heard and continue to develop your own unique voice, what type of people do you hope to attract? What does the group you want to belong to look like?

_____

_____

_____

_____

_____

_____

Have you ever rejected someone because of their differences? How can you grow from that experience?

_____

_____

_____

_____

_____

_____

Creating the Place I Belong

Surrounded by plentiful palms
On this secluded island of mine
Where I sit all alone and think and create
With this God-given light that I shine

Sometimes I am the magnificent Sun
Penetrating light into your days
But you mock my warmth and take it for granted
You are irritated by my rays

Sometimes I am the compassionate Moon
A glimmer of hope when all seems lost
But you're confused by the complexity of all my phases
Using artificial sources, never counting the cost

Sometimes I am the midnight Star
A knowledgeable guide offering direction
But you curse me for sharing the blessing of wisdom
Pushing away my offers of protection

And sometimes I just want to be the grains of sand
Conforming under the pressure of your feet
Doing whatever it is you want me to do
A moment of belonging would feel so complete

And sometimes I just want to be in oneness with the water
Blending quietly with the fluidity of the ocean
A tiny drop among many in rhythm with the tide
Gaining acceptance in the flowing motion

And sometimes I just want to be a palm like you
Swaying in unison with the wind in my face
So I can experience your approval just this once
And the false security provided by your embrace

But here's the thing about the palms
Sometimes they're not really trees at all
Sometimes they're the insides of rejecting hands
Pushing me, shoving me, hoping I'll fall

But I'll not cave in at the sake of my voice
All the world shall hear my song
I'll keep sitting right here on this island of mine
And CREATE the place I belong

CHAPTER 3

<u>WHAT IS VOICE?</u>

Before you were born, people tried to define you. When your mother was pregnant with you, it is very likely that many people she encountered wanted to know if you were a boy or a girl; if would you be breast or bottle fed; how your nursery would be decorated; if you would be pushed toward pink, steered away from it or exposed to a combination of many colors.

These things start to identify you before you are even born. Then the most significant and basic identifier is decided for you...your name. Parents spend months scouring the internet, magazines and baby books in search of the perfect name. And it doesn't end there. Some parents choose names because of their meanings and fully expect their children to live up to them.

But, what if your name means something you're not feeling? Your name may be Daisy, but flowers and springtime don't even come close to describing you. That's okay. You know why? Because once you begin to babble and toddle and experience and grow and express, it is your job to take over that assignment. Your main objective should be to assume control of your identity and begin to attach your own definition to your name. Your environment—your parents, family, friends, spiritual leaders, coaches and educators—should support your desire to do so.

I have spent the vast majority of my life hating my name, Donloyn. It cannot be found in any baby name book or online (unless you're googling me, which I encourage you to do). I'm still unclear as to how my mother's friend talked her into my name.

What's worse is no one can seem to pronounce it. I've been called Donna-Lynn, Don-loin, Dandelion, and even Deedle-bug by my third grade teacher who decided it would be much easier to nickname me. I have had countless individuals ask if there was something else they could call me after declaring there was no possible way they could ever remember how to say it. You would've thought I asked them to pronounce the formal name of the giant protein that scientists call Titan. Its technical name is the longest word in the English dictionary at 189,819 letters long. That's a far cry from my seven-letter name, which, by the way, is pronounced Da-Lawn and rhymes with salon. See, easy. But now, I love my name. It is unique. It is one-of-a-kind. And so am I.

When people don't take the time to learn your name — your most basic and most significant identifier — it can make you feel as if you don't matter. It can make you feel like your name and its meaning are insignificant. Please know, attempts to make you feel small will likely happen to you at some point in your life, if it hasn't already. It doesn't matter if your name is long or short, difficult or easy; there will be people who will attempt to strip your name of its significance and assign it a meaning that does not fairly represent who you are.

Here's the key...you don't have to help them. When you take charge of your identity, when you give your name a positive and purposeful meaning, when you treat your identity with love and respect, you command the same from others. Your confidence and self-assurance will speak volumes.

Now, will your poise and assurance get through to everyone? Of course not. There will always be those few who will buzz with negativity, desperately attempting to drown out your voice. Regardless of the nastiness they bring, they will never be able to reassign meaning to your name as long as you don't allow them. Remain true to your voice, and you will always be in control of your identity.

At this point, you've likely noticed I continue to reference voice and identity. Why? Let's begin with this question: What is voice?

Voice is not just the audible sound that is made when speaking or singing. It's not even just the squeak that caterpillars make when they're afraid (Yes, caterpillars squeak!). It is the person behind that sound. It is your style, your individuality, your presence, your attitude and your expressiveness. It's how you walk; how you talk; how you laugh, smile and dress. It's your talents, your interests and your character. It's what you think and how you communicate those thoughts.

Voice, as I stated earlier, is your identity. And your identity is what makes your story special. Whether you realize it or not, each day you're alive is another page in the narrative you're telling. That is the purpose of your existence...to affect positive change in the lives of others through the telling of your unique story.

Your voice—your identity—makes all the difference in how your story is told. Will you write a heroic account of an inspired, fulfilled life or a painful tragedy filled with disappointments and failures? The way in which you use your voice is how you assign meaning to your name. How will others feel when they hear your name spoken? Will you leave people regretting their encounter with you? Or will you leave a beautiful, lasting impression?

Write your name here.

_____

Do you like your name? Why or why not?

_____

_____

_____

_____

_____

How do you want people to feel when they hear your name?

_____

_____

_____

_____

What meaning do wish to assign your name?

_____

_____

_____

_____

_____

CHAPTER 4

FINDING AND DEFINING VOICE

Although I had this unfulfilled need to be heard and no sense of belonging, my voice still whispered to me. Through feelings of isolation and rejection, I remember seeking and shaping my voice. In retrospect, this is very clear. But at the time, I didn't realize that was what I was doing.

I spent a great deal of time in my room engaged in activities that gave me permission to discover the girl within, or at least present me with opportunities to meet and become comfortable with her.

I listened to a lot of music. The radio and my albums were my escape. The lyrics moved my soul. When no one was in earshot, the hairbrush or curling iron became my microphone. And I would sing and sing.

Songs inspired me and sparked my love of poetry. I would study their lyrics. Whether I read them from the inserts included in the albums or wrote them down while pressing my ear to the speaker of my record player, I would let the words and their meanings transport me to other worlds. Worlds where the girl within didn't feel so filled with doubt.

It was there in my room I began writing poems. No one knew I was writing poetry. I never told anyone. I never even shared a few lines. I believed I was born with no talent—that I wasn't good at anything. So, I wrote in secret, hiding my work in a folder tucked away under my bed. I hid artwork, too. Drawing and sketches, privately stored in that same folder.

It was there in my room I pledged to one day have at least one of my writings published. Even though consciously I didn't think I was good at anything, deep down I always knew who I was, where my talents lay and who I was destined to become.

I didn't see it at the time, but these things were always there. I had no idea I was working on finding my voice. I had no idea I was working on defining myself.

Because of my own experiences, I have come to learn that finding your voice is about defining yourself, and defining yourself is about finding your voice. The two are interwoven.

If finding your voice is so intricately intertwined in the definition of yourself, then what defines you? The answer is YOU! You define you. You are responsible for creating your definition. You say who you are. You are the author of your story.

So how do you go about finding and defining who you are? Like anything worth having, it's a process and it takes time. For me, the path to discovery came through words. And more specifically, poetry. But my path was slow and arduous. Not only did I hide my passion for writing, but at one point I even abandoned it. After about a decade of writing and drawing in silence, I threw away my secret folder. All my thoughts, feelings and expressions were tossed out like yesterday's garbage. For many years I never fully gave myself permission to come forward. I kept the real me hidden…hidden from the world, hidden from myself. It wasn't until I entered my thirties that my love of words came back to me. And I was reminded of that pledge I made to myself.

Your journey does not have to be long and painful. You do not have to ignore your inner voice. You do not have to silence the girl within as I did. That is why poetry is sprinkled throughout these pages…in hopes it will make your whispers too loud to ignore.

Begin by asking yourself the following questions:

Who am I?

_____

_____

_____

Who am I when no one else is around?

_____

_____

_____

What qualities do I like about myself?

_____

_____

_____

What am I passionate about?

_____

_____

_____

What motivates me?

_____

_____

_____

What makes me happy?

_____

_____

_____

What do I stand for?

_____

_____

_____

What will I stand against?

_____

_____

_____

How do I wish to see myself in the world?

_____

_____

_____

If I could be anywhere, where would I be? What would I be
doing?

_____

_____

_____

Honestly asking and answering these questions on a regular basis will help you get to know yourself. As you discover what moves you, your unique voice will emerge. And as you become rooted in your voice, your true identity will shine through.

Your discovery of voice isn't just about knowing what defines you, but also what does not. Identifying the things that do not define you will help preserve a positive self-image. Viewing yourself in a constructive manner will prevent you from handing over the responsibility of assigning yourself meaning.

So what things don't define you? The answer is simple. Any thought, emotion or declaration designed to make you feel inadequate or "less than" does not define you. You are not defined by the opinions, perceptions or prejudgments of others. You are not defined by your friends or any pressure that may exist to fit in. Your mistakes do not define you. You are not defined by doubt, fear, hurt, pain, loss, struggle or shame. These hardships exist to teach us lessons.

When difficult situations present themselves — and they will — it is your obligation to learn from them and not allow them to consume you. If you permit negativity to define you, then you hand over your voice. In doing so, you hand over your authority. Remember, the ultimate goal is to step into your power, *to believe in your wings*. You cannot do that if the first critical element is missing. To step into your power and take flight, you must find and use your voice.

The Girl Within

I heard a whisper,

faint and slim

"Who am I?" said

the girl within

I paid no mind,

still tried to fit in

"Who am I?" sighed

the girl within

Ignorance was bliss,

led by so-called friends,

"Who am I?" called

the girl within

I surrendered my story,

Gave the enemy my pen

"Who am I?" cried

The girl within

A trail of mistakes,
Humiliation and chagrin
"Who am I?" wept
The girl within

I was lost in the world,
Shame and doubt settled in
"Who am I?" bellowed
The girl within

Donned a cloak of toughness,
Masked pain with a grin
And still, "Who am I?" from
The girl within

Tried to silence the pain,
truth wouldn't let me win
then, and unmistakable, "WHO AM I?!" from
the girl within

Her cries were penetrating,
My light had gone dim
And I could no longer ignore
The girl within

So I picked up my journal,
And took back my pen
And I decided to get to know
The girl within

She was made in God's image,
So I sent prayers up to Him
That He would help me be worthy of
The girl within

I listened to her intimate thoughts,
Her wild dreams knew no end
And I was amazed by the talents of
The girl within

We had so much in common,
We liked to paint, dance and swim
And I began to fall in love with
The girl within

Standing in my purpose,
My identity a precious gem
I became almost inseparable from
The girl within

I reflected on what she asked

When she knew I needed a friend

How she would plead, "Who am I?"

How I would reject the girl within

But now the two have become united

You can't tell where she stops and I begin

For she is I, and I am she

I AM THE GIRL WITHIN

CHAPTER 5

<u>DELIVERING VOICE</u>

I wish I could share some profound story about how effectively I delivered my voice when I was younger. The truth is, when I was younger, I was angry and bitter inside. I felt completely alone. I felt no one was fighting for me, so I had to do it for myself. The anger, bitterness and need to protect myself was a direct result of my having been molested and raped at age five. Overcoming an ordeal like that requires years of regular discussions, therapy and monitoring, and affects you differently at different stages of your development. Unfortunately, my parents hoped that I would forget about it and move on with my life. So I didn't get the help I needed.

We may be able to forget the specific details of a horrific event, but the emotions and heartache are always there. Even if the misery of a tragedy is buried deep within our subconscious minds, it is still there. It is still a part of who we are. And when left unaddressed, it manifests. It becomes who we are. It hijacks our psyche and becomes this single, one-dimensional definition of our identity. And that pain becomes the only voice that is delivered.

My voice was anger. I never backed down from a fight, but I wasn't the stereotypical angry teen, rebelling and going a few rounds with an opponent in the hallways between classes. I actually hid my anger quite well. I was nice girl. Friendly. Pleasant. Until someone or something gave me reason not to be. I was loyal, fiercely protective. When a situation threatened my well-being or the well-being of someone I cared about, I would dive into fight-mode. This gave the illusion of strength and confidence.

Maybe I'm being a little unfair to my younger self. I *was* strong. But my strength came from the wrong source. My strength was fueled by my fear. I was a tough girl who was afraid of being hurt. I was the defender of those who were seen as weak and easy targets. To those looking on, I looked as if I had it all together. As if my confidence and self-assurance were intact. But the only thing I was confident in was my determination never to be a victim again.

True strength and confidence should come from a place of knowing. Knowing who you are, why you were created and what your purpose is. This is true for any style of voice. Today, my voice is still one of strength and confidence, but it is no longer delivered in anger. I am still that same loyal, protective defender. The difference now is that I have a positive, proactive approach that is meant to build up others versus a negative, reactive one that only serves to tear down.

So how do you deliver your voice? How do you share your identity, thoughts, ideas and feelings with a world that so often tries to shut you up or drown you out?

First, you have to realize that just because you are delivering your voice doesn't mean someone will or even has to receive it. You are not in control of anyone else. You are in control of you and you alone. To be heard is a wonderful gift. Listening is a beautiful expression of love and respect. However, listening is a choice. If someone chooses not to hear your voice, then all you can do is allow them that freedom. But you must remember that their choice not to listen should never dictate whether or not you express yourself and who you are.

Your voice can be shared in so many unique ways. Perhaps you are an artist with a passion for painting. Or a singer blessed with the gift of song. Maybe you're an athlete who not only strives to achieve her absolute best, but also encourages others to do the same. The masterpieces you create; the melodies you compose; the records you break…all of these are reflections of your gifting, interests and passions. Where these talents and motivations lie is where you go to tap into your identity and deliver your unique message. Go to your special place of inspiration and share your voice from that space. That is where your authentic self resides. Never share it from the place where negativity, anger, bitterness and pain reside. That's the place of fear, and there is no authenticity in that.

Don't get me wrong. If you are feeling angry, fearful and hurt, those are real emotions. And you have every right to convey and express them. There is no rule that says you are only allowed to share happy thoughts. That's unrealistic and will only alter your voice. If you're feeling negative emotions, allow them to inspire a beautiful creation. Share the pain. Share the hurt. But share it in a way that lifts you up and encourages others. Share it in a way that inspires thought and brings forth change. Never share undesirable emotions for the purpose of hurting or destroying. Instead, use the negativity to your advantage. Let it fuel your voice.

As you develop your identity — your unique voice — remember these three things:

1. You say who you are.
2. Your voice is a thing of beauty.
3. When you share your gifting, interests and passions, you share your voice.

Who do **YOU** say you are? Remember, your answer is not limited to the "who" you are now. You can also share the "who" you wish to become. There is power in words. So speak who you are and who you will be, and it will happen!

_____

_____

_____

_____

_____

_____

_____

_____

What are some of your special talents, gifts and interests?

_____

_____

_____

_____

_____

_____

_____

_____

How do you or how can you use them to share your voice and express your identity?

_____

_____

_____

_____

_____

_____

_____

_____

What negative emotion/emotions have you allowed to influence your voice?

_____

_____

_____

_____

_____

_____

_____

_____

_____

How can you use it/them to your advantage in the future?

_____

_____

_____

_____

_____

_____

_____

_____

_____

_____

Screaming Against the Wind

Remember that day I was standing outside
Tears in my eyes, a deep pain inside
You didn't pass me by
You acknowledged each sigh, heard my every cry
You knew I needed a friend
When you saw me screaming...
Screaming against the wind

The ones who were supposed to didn't seem to care
Trapped in their snare, unjust and unfair
You untangled my hair
Encouraged me to share, allowed my soul to bear
You knew I needed a friend
When you saw me screaming...
Screaming against the wind

For years and a year, needing a compassionate ear
Instead met by misery and fears
My voice was smothered, inaudible and unclear
My thoughts drowned in bitter tears
My spirit was broken, I could no longer bend
And I stood there screaming...
Screaming against the wind

Didn't want to be a victim, didn't want to pretend

But it was hard to blend in when my wounds wouldn't

mend

"Are you hearing my voice yet?" Chances were quite slim

Identity threatened, future looked grim

"When will my silence end?"

And I stood there screaming...

Screaming against the wind

You took me by the shoulders,

your words strong and wise

And turned me to change my direction,

much to my surprise

A beacon to light the darkest days

lay there before my eyes

The coveted prize

behind me the entire time

My revelation sublime

All that was heard was silence...

Silence and the wind

"Shift focus, change directions,

don't let it kill your fire

Turn around, use it wisely,

let it propel you higher and higher

Fighting against what's natural

will cause your spirit to tire

Dig deeply, shine brightly,

become all you aspire."

Wind against my back, my treasure chest wide opened

My jewels spread across the earth with every word spoken

Now that I was screaming...

Screaming WITH the wind

STAGE II

COURAGE

THE CHRYSALIS

CHAPTER 6

UNDERSTANDING FEAR

After I was molested, I began having horrible nightmares. I was haunted. As a result, I developed a fear of the dark. I struggled with that fear for many years. On many nights, I would awaken from a bad dream and scan the room frantically. I was certain that the shadows and outlines of objects around me were moving.

During that time, I struggled with a recurring nightmare. That struggle continued for many years. In my slumber, with no particular regularity, the boogeyman would come to visit. He wasn't raised with manners. He never called before he came. Never announced his visits. He would just show up and he knew exactly when to come calling to interrupt my attempts to salvage my innocence. Each time he came, he terrorized me — creating the whirring buzz, frightening my inner caterpillar, shaking me from my chrysalis — because developing and spreading my beautiful wings would surely mean the death of him.

On the nights of his unannounced visits, I would close my eyes and, unknowingly, enter a world of deception. A world of seclusion and lies hidden beneath the guise of happiness and truth. In that world, I'm a little girl. I'm at ease…content…in perfect peace. I'm sitting on the floor in a bright room. The sun is beaming in, and I'm playing. By myself. Happily. On the floor. With an empty cardboard box.

The entire room is bare. Perhaps, we're moving. Out or in, I do not know. It's just empty. No furniture. No carpeting. No wall hangings. Nothing. Just me, hardwood floors, the cardboard box, happiness and the front door. The door is open.

Without warning, the mood changes. The room darkens. There is no more light. No more happiness. Only fear. Horror sweeps across me. I'm young. Innocent. Alone. Unprotected. I leap from the floor and run towards the open door, but not to exit. To shut it. To close myself in. To keep him out. I need to keep him out. Away. Away from me. No one else can do it. No one else is around. No one else knows. I must protect myself.

Oh my God, he's coming! Hurry! Run faster, little girl! Run faster! Get to the door before he does!

I get to the door. I begin to shut it. It's almost closed. *BANG!* There's a slamming force against the other side. *NO!* It's him! He's here! He's pushing against the door. Pushing against me. He's trying to get in. He's trying to get to me. All he wants is me. He wants to devour me. It's his ritual. One I know all too well.

I'm pushing against the door with all my might, but I am only five; I am no match for him. I am no match for his strength. His appetite for my innocence is too powerful.

As I struggle to shut the door completely, I see his face in the gap. It is distorted. Scrambled. Blocked out as if the television news is concealing his identity during an interview. I can't make out his face, but I know who he is. I may not be able to escape him, but he cannot fool me.

The struggle continues in silence. There is no sound at all in this dream. Not even when I am happy and playful. But then, I hear something. No, someone. Someone filled with anguish. It is me. It is the muffled heaviness of my breath. It is dreadful and panting. This part is not a dream. I wake up.

Panic-stricken, I shake and cry.

I wonder...*why me? God, why did this have to happen to me?*

I would relive this recurring nightmare for the next 11 years. The same haunting visit, again and again, with nothing changing. Nothing changing, except the little girl having the dream. With each passing year, that little girl, lying awake and alone in her room, slowly evolved from a five-year-old girl to a teenager. I never knew when that nightmare would visit me in my sleep. I never knew if there was something in particular that triggered it. I lived in fear. In fear of the dark. In fear of the light. In fear of remembering. In fear of forgetting. In fear of him.

As a result of this constant horror, I slept with a bedside lamp on for a while. That is, until a bully brother-sister team who lived across the street from me noticed the light was always shining from my bedroom window. They started to tease me about needing the light on to sleep. One time, I lied and said, "I don't use a night light. I just happen to fall asleep while reading my bible." I know. Whack response, but what else was I supposed to say? I couldn't let them see my irrational fear.

When I was 16, the nightmare stopped. I'll explain why it stopped in the next chapter. But even now as a grown woman, that old childhood fear of the dark can come creeping back in. From time-to-time, I find myself feeling that same anxiety deep in the darkness of the night. That's because fear is a learned emotion. And if we follow the trail of most unpleasant emotions, we find they usually lead to some type of learned fear. Each time I expressed my voice through anger and bitterness, I was demonstrating what I had learned. I was terrified of being hurt again, so I learned to protect myself and those I loved through rage and aggression. Those two emotions are deeply rooted in fear.

It's important to know that fear itself is not a bad emotion. Although it has the reputation of being this undesirable thing, it's not. After all, you are learning. And learning is a good thing. The key is choosing how and what you learn from the experience. It isn't the fear that can be detrimental; it's your response to it.

Some fears are rational. They offer us protection. This type of fear develops as a result of something unfavorable that has happened to us. In those cases, it is a learned behavior designed to protect you from suffering or reliving an undesirable experience. Much like the caterpillar confuses the wasps and the bees, we typically end up interpreting the fear incorrectly. The better we understand our fears, the more in control we can be of our responses to them.

For example, it wasn't really the dark I was afraid of. It was what the dark represented and what could happen to me there. I was fearful of being hurt again. I was fearful of reliving that torment in the form of nightmares. Suffering through the pain of molestation and rape is a horrifying ordeal for child. So it makes perfect sense that I wanted to safeguard myself after having endured such an assault. It's rational to avoid being harmed in that way again. But to blame the dark is not. This is why it is important to understand our fears and to respond to them appropriately. Otherwise, they get out of hand and become phobias that control the direction of our lives.

Rational fear is the fear we begin to learn as babies. It keeps us safe. After becoming closely bonded with those who provide them care, babies will demonstrate a fear of being separated from those individuals. They learn the faces and personalities of those who feed and love them. They know their survival depends on that type of care. So when the ones they depend on are not around, they cry. Eventually, most babies learn that mommy and daddy are coming back, and there is no need to fear. Thus, no need to cry. It's all a process. A rational process of learning, understanding and choosing your response.

As babies begin to explore their environments, they learn to fear heights and steep edges. They learn to stay away from hot objects and power outlets. By either associating the distress from an actual incident or the discomfort from hearing a startling "NO!" when they come close to one of these dangers, babies develop these rational fears that protect and preserve their wellbeing.

Conversely, some fears are irrational. Instead of offering us sensible protection, they become phobias designed to paralyze us. These are the fears that hold us back. They keep us from growing. It is important to note that some rational fears can quickly become irrational ones if we choose to feed the fear versus face it. When we choose to surrender to these irrational fears, we are saying that we are at peace with being limited and placed in tiny, ever-shrinking boxes. We are saying that we are willing to accept a life sentence of living in the comfort zone, never knowing challenges or the potential victories that could accompany those challenges. Why would any of us ever choose to be okay with that? Why would we choose to live a life void of the opportunity to celebrate accomplishments and moments of greatness? Victory can only exist after something has been conquered.

For many years, I was consumed by irrational fear. My biggest fear was the fear of anyone finding out that I had been raped and molested. I hid in silence with this dirty secret and the illogical notion that I would be ostracized should anyone find out what I had been hiding. This fear stemmed from learned behavior. My parents had hoped I would forget about the terror I experienced, so they remained silent. There were no discussions with me about what happened or what I may have been feeling as a result. This silence, though the intention was good, crippled me. It became a playground for emotions of shame, guilt, disgust, self-hate and loneliness. The more my parents remained quiet, the more I remained quiet. Eventually, I interpreted this silence as validation of these unhealthy emotions, and I concluded I was never to speak of my situation to anyone.

As I grew older, this fear worsened. Mean-spirited peers began to comment negatively on my mixed African and European lineage. They told me I was the result of rape. They said I was the slave master's daughter. That my entire existence was due to my female ancestors being violated by hateful slave owners. After hearing these ugly words, I was convinced more than ever that keeping my silence was the only way.

This silence had a tremendous impact on my voice, which resulted in damage to my courage. Choosing to remain silent stemmed from the Longing to Belong. We all want to feel liked and accepted. We want to feel as though we fit. But everything around me was telling me that if I revealed my truth, I would never fit in. In hiding my story, I was conforming. In my silence, I was honoring the need to belong over the need to be heard. That desperate shift from boldly sharing your voice to desperately hiding your truth to please others opens the door for a life ruled by fear. This silence…this fear…had great power because I was surrendering my own. Each day that I lived in secrecy was another day of feeding it. And as I fed it, it grew and grew. And the more this fear grew, the longer the nightmare and fear of the dark persisted. I was choosing to surrender to the fear. Choosing to allow it to hold me hostage.

Read the last two sentences again. Notice I used the word "choose." Fear can only hold you back if you allow it. It's your choice. You can choose to allow irrational paranoias direct the course of your life, or you can stand tall at the helm, facing every swell that comes rolling your way.

What does Fear mean to you?

_____

_____

_____

_____

_____

_____

What are some things that cause you to feel fear?

_____

_____

_____

_____

_____

_____

What is your biggest fear? From where does it stem?

_____

_____

_____

_____

_____

_____

How do you handle it?

_____

_____

_____

_____

_____

_____

Has irrational fear ever prevented you from doing
something you really wanted to experience? Explain.

_____

_____

_____

_____

_____

Is there a part of you you're hiding for fear of someone
seeing or knowing you for who you really are?

_____

_____

_____

_____

Have these questions sparked any additional thoughts you'd like to explore? This book belongs to you…don't be afraid to share your thoughts here. This is your safe space.

_____

_____

_____

_____

_____

_____

_____

_____

Hiding in Open Spaces

hiding in open spaces

tucked away in plain sight

among others, friends, strangers, people

among birds and butterflies taking flight

among the green grass, fluffy clouds, blue skies

standing next to beauty and possibility

watching opportunities pass me by

i am there hiding

present in the midst of it all

unnoticed, concealed, quiet

hidden behind a secrecy wall

veiled, cloaked, covered, invisible

paralyzed, still, afraid

silent, hiding in plain sight

torment casting a shade

no one seeing what is buried so deeply

hidden with exact precision

hidden so well it's staring them in their faces

shame made that decision

all they see is a smile

the smile i painted on yesterday

i'll never show them my tears

but inside i am crying out restlessly

it's a breathless, voiceless cry

untouchable possibilities too intense to bear

the fear, the pain, this secret keeps me bound

with dreams and hopes forbidden to share

it won't let me give life

won't let me create

torture envelops me

and I'm too afraid

too afraid to reveal

afraid to raise my beautiful voice

i mustn't confess, expose or speak

fear is my only choice

my tongue is paralyzed

my feet planted tight

my heart can't dream

my pen won't write

my story rests there in the center of it all

under your nose of all places

untold

unspoken

unwritten

unread

it is there…

hiding in open spaces

CHAPTER 7

<u>CHOOSING COURAGE</u>

Being able to identify your fear is important. It is the first step in overcoming it. Fear is not something that should be avoided. It's a real emotion. It is a part of you, and it deserves acknowledgment and respect. What it does not deserve is a voice. Your fears should have no say or influence in how you move forward in your life.

When in the presence of fear, we can either allow it to paralyze us or to push us forward. Fear is generally the biggest obstacle for most people, but you must use that fear as fuel. Allow it to challenge you. Face it head on. Chase it down if you have to. Once it is in your grasp, remind it that its only function is to serve as your cue to initiate courage. Use it as a gauge. If you're facing a new opportunity for growth and you begin to experience fear, use that feeling as confirmation to move forward. Let that feeling be an indicator that you must do that thing. Allow it to push you in the direction of your dreams. If something scares you, then that's all the more reason to go after it. You are on a journey to personal power. Conquered fears are simply the stepping stones on your path to greatness.

I've had many moments when I gave into the fear...moments when I was unable move forward. In those moments, I clung to the false security of my comfort zone and, as a result, there were missed opportunities that quickly transformed into regret. When we choose fear, we are paving the path to remorse and wasted potential. We are saying *No* to courage and, thus, closing the door on any chances for victory.

Conversely, there have also been successful moments. Pivotal moments when I trusted my gifting and chose to begin something new. In those moments, the fear was great, but the warrior in me proved greater. As each fear was identified, stared in the face and conquered, a new stepping stone was placed at my feet and another positive step was taken toward fulfilling my purpose.

How then do you conquer fear? How do you overcome it? The answer is by choosing courage. Courage is the ultimate weapon against fear. But in order to choose courage, you must first explore what it is and how it is cultivated.

Courage, by definition, is that mental or spiritual quality that gives us the strength and moral fortitude to face, combat and overcome difficulties and challenges despite the fear they bring. Courage is recognizing a danger, but choosing to stand tall in the midst of it. Courage is dancing your way through the raging waters even though the waves are beating against you.

But courage is even more than that. It is the single most important attribute that any individual can possess. It lies at the heart of everything we do. Anything that involves taking a risk requires courage to be done well. To love, to believe, to give, to trust, to dream, to create, to forgive, to express, to share…everything. All of these things require courage because they each involve taking a risk. The risk of failure, rejection or pain. The risk of facing an undesirable outcome. The risk of things not turning out the way we had hoped. When you fall in love, it takes courage to express that love. When you create a beautiful painting, it takes courage to share your creativity. When you think you have the correct answer, it takes courage to raise your hand in class and respond. It even takes courage to read this book. By reading this book and participating in its activities, you are demonstrating the desire and willingness to examine your innermost thoughts, to make painful adjustments and difficult decisions, if necessary, and to create an opening for personal growth. And that takes courage.

But courage must be developed. It has to be planted, watered, cared for and cultivated. You develop courage not by simply choosing it, but also by recognizing that each time you choose it, you are giving it the opportunity to mature. Courage is unique in that the more you use it, the more you have. Each courageous act lends itself to the next and so on. It's like a muscle. The more it is exercised…the more it is taxed…the more it is pushed beyond its limits, the stronger that muscle becomes and the more weight it can carry and endure.

It wasn't until high school that I made my first step toward breaking the silence that had been holding me hostage for so long. And if I am to be completely honest, it was because a situation arose that made me feel as though I had to offer an explanation for my behavior.

I started dating the cousin of one of my best friends. He was one of the kindest, most genuine people I've ever known. Friendly, warm smile, compassionate, respectful. And he treated me like a lady. There was one slight drawback…he shared the same surname as my abuser. Fortunately, I was able to quickly get past that fact, as that particular last name is quite common. In fact, it was my grandmother's maiden name. So, I let it go.

That is until I found out his brother had the exact same first name as my attacker. Yes, my boyfriend's brother shared the same first and last names as the teenage boy who had molested, manipulated, threatened and raped me. That was a heavy detail I just couldn't get over.

I began to pull away from him. It didn't matter what a good person he was. It didn't matter how funny or kind. All I could think of when I was around him was the very thing I was trying to forget. And so, I broke things off. However, I was still close friends with his cousin, and, for the sake of our friendship, I felt I owed her an explanation. I was fearful of losing her friendship. I just couldn't bear the thought of allowing my abuser to take anything else away from me.

So, at the risk of being looked upon with disgust, I chose courage and took a chance on our friendship. I made the decision to trust the bond we had formed. I mustered up the strength, and I told her my story. The abridged version, but still my story, nonetheless. I explained how difficult it was to know that my ex-boyfriend's brother carried the same name…how it felt too close to me…too much of a burden that I was simply unwilling and ill-equipped to carry.

She understood. She didn't judge me. She didn't think the abuse I suffered tarnished me. She didn't deem me unworthy. I took a risk, and she and I are still friends today.

She was the first person I ever told. I often wonder if she remembers my telling her…if she knew then how difficult my opening up was. It took a great deal of courage to allow myself to be vulnerable, to open up and risk rejection. Breaking my silence has been a long, complex journey. It has been sporadic, emotional and has even caused family upset. But it has led to the development of my voice and courage. It has also cultivated a passion in me for encouraging others to share their personal narratives and grow their courage, as well.

In my case, courage came by way of me breaking my silence. Each time I shine a light on my past pain, share my truth and use my experiences as teachable moments, I choose courage. Writing this book for you takes courage. Courage is a heavy hitter. It ruffles feathers. It shakes things up. It pulls issues that most are not brave enough to face to the forefront. It starts discussions and inspires thought. It creates connection, understanding and solutions. Courage is powerful.

Sharing my truth with my friend that day made it easier to share small bits of my story with another trusted friend, and then another. By allowing myself to be vulnerable, I took the first steps towards authentic courage and personal strength. When I faced that which made me weak, I discovered a power that allowed me to share it again and again. That power, the power that comes from attacking fears head on, is the feeling of courage growing…multiplying.

After I shared my story with my friend that day, I never had the recurring nightmare again. I let someone in…into the space I had been carefully hiding. And as a result, I broke the haunting cycle of complete loneliness. I have often wished to have that nightmare again, to have the unwelcomed intruder pay me one of his unannounced visits. Not because I want to be frightened, but because I want to see the little girl win. I want to see the five-year-old me stand tall and brave. I want to give her the opportunity to choose courage. I want to see her victory. I want HER to see her victory. And who knows…perhaps, one night I will get that chance.

Think of the situation that is causing you the most fear. Write it down. Now recognize your emotions when you think of that thing. Do you feel anxiety? Butterflies in your stomach? Shaky? Sweaty palms? Heart racing?

_____

_____

_____

_____

_____

_____

_____

Is this the fear of seizing an opportunity? Or is this a fear of facing an obstacle?

_____

_____

_____

_____

Now move past the negative emotions…think of how you will feel if you decide to do that thing or remove that obstacle. What you should be searching for is a feeling of victory. What do you need to do to feel brave and accomplished in the face of this fear? What's your plan of attack?

_____

_____

_____

_____

_____

_____

How will you feel after you've put your plan into action and it turns out well?

_____

_____

_____

_____

_____

What if it doesn't turn out well? (HINT: If it doesn't turn out well, you have NOT failed. You have demonstrated bravery, and that is a WIN!)

_____

_____

_____

_____

Now, how will you feel if you don't face it at all? How will you feel if you choose fear, abandon courage, turn your back on bravery and allow the opportunity to pass or the obstacle to win?

_____

_____

_____

_____

_____

_____

You are capable of demonstrating great courage. You must only choose to take action. To stand tall in the face of fear. To dance through the difficult times even when your knees are shaking. Choose courage. Recognize the fear, but choose courage and do that thing anyway. Tell fear to take a seat...you've got wings to grow!

I'll Dance

When you gaze upon my withered skin
Casting judgments
As if you know where I've been,
I'll Dance...Even Then, I'll Dance

When my peculiar stillness makes you jeer
Scoffing my intelligence
Instilling fear
I'll Dance...Even Then, I'll Dance

When you say nothing I touch will ever thrive
In your eyes I am barren
But inside I remain alive
I'll Dance...Even Then, I'll Dance

When life's challenges have beat me down
Unloved and unwanted
Crying tears of a clown
I'll Dance...Even Then, I'll Dance

When the forces working against me, devise a treacherous
scheme
The elements, in all their grandeur, become my enemies

When the sun burns, beaming down, upon my weathered
and blistered flesh

In this scorching, fiery furnace, I flail about and thresh

When the wind joins in the pounding, blowing, throwing,
hurling

Causing a sandstorm of pain and hurt, and the oppression
has me whirling

When the tide steps in, with its constant phases

Rising, drowning me, falling, exposing me, confusing me
with all these changes

When the waves take center stage, crashing and thrashing
against me

I retreat far within my twisted dry skin, in my sanctuary I
hide deeply

When the sand shifts beneath my feet, bringing me
instability

When I dig in deeper, holding on tighter, despite the
uncertainty

I'll Dance...Even Then, I'll Dance

It's my toughened exterior that has allowed me to endure

Because of my hurts, I'm stronger

My heart is powerful; my soul triumphant

I know defeat no longer

The beauty, love and joy in my heart

Create a harmonious symphony

The trumpets and harps of angels collide

I dance as they serenade me

As I sway, spin and arabesque with each test

The trials become so easy

Throw at me what you will, do to me as you wish

Your doubt can no longer defeat me

I'll Dance...Even Then, I'll Dance

Even though the sun with its powerful rays

Burns me with its heat

When the hard day is done, I am granted reprieve

The torture stops, it retreats

The moon appears and cools my burns

Bringing with it twinkles of promise

Giving me time to dance with my dreams

A hope for a better tomorrow

In the morning, the sun will undoubtedly return

Bringing with it every conspirator

But I'll be waiting, with grace and elegance

Me, the beautiful dancer...

And I'll Dance...Even Then I'll Dance

CHAPTER 8

CHANGING MINDSET AND MEANINGS

Understanding fear and choosing courage is always easier when we have the proper mindset. Our mindset is our attitude toward concepts, ideas, people and things. It's our way of thinking about the world around us.

Dr. Wayne Dyer, a world renowned spiritual and inspirational author and speaker, said, "Change the way you look at things and the things you look at change." We have more power over our thoughts and perceptions than we realize. By simply changing your mind about something—changing the way you look at it or think about it—you can completely change the outcome of that situation.

Mindsets are shaped by experiences. Our experiences directly affect how we define and respond to the things that enter into our personal spaces. If we have a good experience, we are likely to look at that situation favorably. Unfortunately, not all of our encounters are positive or healthy. As a result, our way of thinking about certain realities can become flawed. In these instances, we allow negative or undesirable events to shape our perceptions. In order to understand fear and respond to that fear with courage, we must correct our mindsets and begin assigning new meanings to concepts that affect us most. We have to look at those things *differently*. And that takes a conscious effort and a great deal of practice.

An adjustment in mindset can also make it easier to forgive a wrong or cope with a hardship you have suffered. When we choose to look at our offender and the offense with new eyes, it can help us let go of the pain and bitterness associated with that hurtful experience. It can also make it easier to feel compassion for that individual. When we look at the wrongdoings of others in a new light, we develop the ability to see the hurt and pain they may have endured. It is likely that the difficulties they have endured have negatively impacted their mindsets. This causes fear to develop in them, making it easier to lash out against you. I don't say this to make excuses for bad behavior. I don't say this to let hurtful people off the hook. I say this so that you never allow another person's inappropriate choices have power over you. Having the proper mindset keeps control where it belongs…in your hands.

When I changed my mindset about my story of sexual abuse, the bitterness, resentment and confusion I carried all those years seemed to wash away. And quite literally. One morning, while taking a shower, thoughts just seemed to pour over me. I wondered what terrible things must have happened to my abuser that resulted in him embarking upon this life as a sex offender. You don't just wake up and decide to make a career of sexually abusing others. Something tragic has to happen first. I wondered if he, too, was sexually abused. I wondered who his offender was. I imagined him as a little child being hurt repeatedly. I knew exactly how that felt, and I pitied him. I thought how vacant his life must have been…void of love, direction and wisdom.

Filled with emotion, I began to pray and cry. And for the first time, I was not only able to forgive my offender but also able to pray for him. I was even able to forgive and pray for his mother and older brother for their roles in my pain, for allowing him continuous access to me and turning a blind eye to his damaging behavior. It was then that I realized I had made significant progress in my healing journey.

Don't misinterpret this. His behavior was vile and disgusting. It completely changed the course of my life. But I will not allow his sins and the destruction they caused control me or prevent me from living a life filled with happiness, promise and hope. I changed my mindset by allowing my pain to fuel my purpose. By deciding to use for good the exact thing that was meant to destroy me, I reclaimed the power that was taken from me. Every stumbling block that was placed on my path has led me to where I am today...here...writing this book, sharing wisdom and life lessons with you. And in that regard, I win.

Your mindset is very powerful. Much like fear, it can either limit you or be the very thing that sets you free. It can mean the difference between walking away from a situation being insightful or being spiteful. It simply depends on how you choose to use it. Let's take a moment to assign new meanings to a couple of key concepts. Afterwards, you'll be invited to explore other topics more personal to you that may be in need of a re-think. Perhaps a fresh mindset in these areas will help you as you bravely navigate through your own personal thoughts, experiences and fears.

Comfort Zones

This concept is referred to when people refuse to take a risk, try something new, face a fear or activate their courage. *"She was too afraid to leave her comfort zone."* But what is this comfort zone, really? Is it some lovely place where nothing ever goes wrong? A place where all is right with the world? A place filled with sunshine and happiness? Not really. In fact, not usually. Your comfort zone simply refers to whatever experiences, emotions, people, places and things you are accustomed to having in your world. The same world that has likely exposed you to hurt, pain, rejection, loss or some other unfortunate circumstance. The same world that has exposed you to fear and has encouraged you to respond to that fear in an irrational manner. The same world where you are being bullied or called names. The same world where you have experienced sexual, verbal or mental abuse. The same world in which you don't fit. The same world where you are experiencing or have experienced whatever hardship or difficulty you have had to endure. Does that sound like comfort?

Life can be pretty chaotic. How is it that we convince ourselves that amid all of that chaos lies our comfort zone? If we are honest with ourselves, we can easily admit that there really isn't much comfort happening in this place. In fact, there is far more fear, dread and doubt going on here than anything else. So why do we feel safe here? There is no safety in fear. There is no comfort in pain. We should be able to walk away from that which holds us back with ease, but instead, we fear the unknown. We fear stepping out of the so-called "comfort zone" because we do not know what lies ahead.

But, like the caterpillar finds refuge in its chrysalis, we too should find comfort and solace in the unknown. We should find comfort in the fact that we are opening the door for progress. When the caterpillar spins its chrysalis, it doesn't know what's to come. All it has ever known since it hatched from an egg is the eating of leaves in its caterpillar state. It has never spun a chrysalis before. It simply trusts that it must happen.

You are the caterpillar, and you must trust that leaving the "comfort zone" and attempting new things is necessary for your growth and development. You must be willing to spin your chrysalis, to choose courage, to venture into the unknown, to face your fears, to take a chance. Each time you demonstrate bravery, you assign new meaning to an experience or situation. And for each moment you choose bravery, your courage grows. Courage grows in the chrysalis.

Fearless versus Courageous

We often hear the word fearless tossed around. It literally means *without fear*. But how realistic is this word? Fear indicates the presence of an opportunity for growth. When we acknowledge our fears and then make the conscious decision to face them, we are demonstrating courage, solidifying our identities and unlocking our personal power. If we are without fear...if we are fearless...if we never recognize teachable moments or opportunities for growth...if we never stretch ourselves beyond our limits or strive for what seems to be unattainable goals, how then will we ever demonstrate bravery? How will we ever know courage? How will we ever experience victory?

We are imperfect humans; therefore, fear exists. It's a natural part of life. But victory comes when we recognize fear exists and make the bold decision to demonstrate bravery anyway. Where there is no fear, there is no challenge and thus no growth. So, again, why would we ever want to be fearless?

Furthermore, when the world tells us to be fearless or not to be afraid, it sends mixed messages and adds undue pressure. It can cause us to question ourselves. To wonder why we are feeling anxiety. To wonder why we are experiencing fear and why we lack the ability to shut it off. *What's wrong with me? They keep telling me not to be afraid, but I am?*

It can also cause us to feel as though our fears and the emotions surrounding those fears aren't valid. This fills us with doubt, which leads to more fear. This type of fear is likely to become irrational and inevitably hold us back from experiencing greatness.

Instead of using the word fearless, let's use the word courageous. By using the word courageous, we automatically acknowledge that we are powerful, courage-filled beings. We also validate our feelings. We tell ourselves it is perfectly okay to experience moments of fright and dread. That it is not those emotions that define us, but our responses to them. You aren't an emotional wreck because you experience fear. You are emotionally intelligent because you admit those fears exist and you handle them accordingly. Being courageous means being in control. It means recognizing, acknowledging and feeling the fear, but standing tall and brave against it anyway. Don't be fearless. Be courageous!

When we let go of old mindsets and allow more productive thought processes to influence us in new ways, we become inspired. The simple act of changing our minds for the better results in us feeling powerful and encouraged. It becomes easier to let go of unnecessary fear, past pain and restrictive rules. You are no longer held captive by blame, hurt and rejection. The intimidation, confusion and powerlessness are no more. You realize the wounded little girl is just an illusion, a façade created by lies and deception. When you let go of old outlooks, the limiting beliefs and destructive attitudes of others no longer have power over you. When you change your mindset and assign new meanings to the thoughts and ideas that once dragged you down, you are breaking free. And that takes courage.

What is your take on the concept of the Comfort Zone? Have you ever been guilty of clinging to this false sense of security? Do you think this new way of looking at it will help you step away from your safety net and experience new things?

_____

_____

_____

_____

_____

_____

_____

_____

_____

In our language, the words *fearless* and *courageous* are typically used synonymously. How do you feel about the differences I highlighted? Do you agree that these two words carry two different meanings?

_____

_____

_____

_____

_____

_____

_____

_____

_____

What are somethings going on in your own world that may

need to be redefined or viewed differently? Is there a

particular situation that has filled you with negative

thoughts and attitudes? If so, how can you change your

mind about that situation? How can you shift your mindset

and regain control?

_____

_____

_____

_____

_____

_____

_____

_____

_____

_____

_____

_____

_____

_____

_____

_____

_____

What is something you'd like to change your mind about,
but just can't seem to do it, yet? What are you not ready to
look at differently?

_____

_____

_____

_____

_____

_____

_____

_____

_____

_____

Today I Changed My Mind

Today I changed my mind about you
And it brought me inner peace
I let go of all the pain in the past
And surprisingly found release
I see my world much differently
Than I did just yesterday
The confusion had a hold on me
Distracted, I lost my way
Life has richer meaning now
All things seem brand new
No longer seeking comfort in fear
Like I did when I had no clue
Now I see that fear is needed
To ignite a courageous mission
A change of heart and a change of mind
Has given me clearer vision
Your grip cannot control me
The way it used to in the past
Your sins and lies have no place here
I am no longer in your grasp
Today I changed my mind about you
And it brought me joy beyond measure
I have no idea what the future holds
But I can't wait to discover its treasure

CHAPTER 9

GROWTH IN THE DARK PLACES

After the caterpillar has completed its job of feeding itself and has become fully grown, it roams about in search of a safe place in which to begin its transformation. Once the perfect spot is found, the caterpillar attaches itself and begins to shed its skin for the last time revealing a wet, silky covering — its chrysalis. The caterpillar is now a pupa, and the chrysalis begins to harden.

Miraculous changes occur within the chrysalis. Hormones and enzymes are released, and tissues that once made up the caterpillar's body begin to melt. The nutrient-rich broth that is formed as a result of this tissue breakdown will serve as the building blocks of the elaborate creature that will soon emerge. Within this *dark place of isolation and messiness*, miraculous changes occur, and growth is underway.

People often shy away from the *dark places of isolation and messiness*, thinking that nothing good can come from being there…spiritually, mentally and emotionally speaking. We are taught that "darkness" is bad…that it should be avoided at all cost. But the use of the word "darkness" is simply a way of classifying life's tough circumstances and situations.

And the emotions that accompany these dark spells are real and deserve their due attention. Instead of dealing with the darkness...the hardships, loneliness, difficulties, confusion, pain, drama, desperation, unhappiness or uncertainty... instead of being willing to sit within the darkness, process their emotions, choose courage and grow, most people would rather avoid it. They'd rather label it as bad.

But, as evidenced by the caterpillar in its chrysalis, good things can happen in the dark. As long as we are willing to be transformed by it. Sometimes, it is necessary to be hidden, to be encased in a protective shell, while chaos, disarray and darkness surround you. It is necessary to experience difficulties, fears, hurts and disappointments so that the uncertain, doubtful you can be *broken down* and *pieced back together* in perfect, beautiful order. And like the butterfly breaking from its chrysalis, you will emerge strong and powerful.

This is where your renewed mindset steps in. In order for this chrysalis process to be successful, you must be willing to see the dark places as opportunities to grow your courage. Those who go through hard times and challenges without searching for wisdom, deciphering the lesson or seeking the potential are missing their chrysalis moments. Life comes with difficulties. We experience a range of emotions. That includes the less popular ones like sadness, hurt, regret, brokenness and loneliness. There's no getting around that. But, in order to create a new and improved you, you must learn to piece together your messy bits. That work must be done in the darkness.

Sometimes, you must dwell in the darkness in order to see and appreciate the light…to see that tiny glimmer that's already shining within you…to hone in on it and grow it into a brilliant beacon for all to see. Darkness doesn't have to be this scary place. And it certainly isn't meant to be your permanent home. It's temporary. It's where we deal with the hard stuff. It's the battleground. It's where the unknown, the uncertain, the unchartered and absence exist. It's where we go to roll up our sleeves and do the real work. It's where change, transformation and evolution occur. It's the birthplace of courage. Metamorphosis happens in the dark places.

The chrysalis is rare and unique, as no other living thing goes through this. The same can be said for you. You are unique. Your journey…your story…your transformation from a doubt-filled girl to a confident and powerful young woman is unique. At times, you may feel you are a complete mess on the inside. You're not. Just as the caterpillar is reduced to a nutrient-filled slush that will take on a new shape and form, your "mess" is a process of sorting emotions and feelings and a rebuilding of character and fortitude. This process of putting back together will form your wings.

Just as the caterpillar is *broken down* by the enzymes that are designed to digest and *melt* its tissue, certain situations will melt you into a puddle of emotion—a soup of nothingness filled with questions, fear, uncertainty and despair. Don't lose hope. When you are in the dark places, recognize the potential for growth. Recognize it as a time and place of transformation…transitioning and morphing into something new. When you're in the dark places, do the work. Sit with the emotion. Analyze your thoughts, and adjust your mindset. Face your fears head on. Choose courage, and build those powerful wings.

This chrysalis process will occur every time you embark upon life's challenges. But it is solely up to you to take advantage of the opportunities that come along with it. Occasions to strengthen your character only present themselves in situations where you are being tested, hard-pressed and challenged. While you're navigating your way through it, it gets messy. It's intricate. It's detailed. You have to be willing to do the work…to allow the changes to take place…to understand that it must happen in order to emerge strong, powerful, bold and brand new. This metamorphosis is not a beautiful process. It's the end result that's beautiful.

Each time you make the choice to take on a fear, learn from a hurt or process pain, you are stepping into your chrysalis, into the dark place, and you are growing your courage. And when the process is complete — when you've slain that fear, when you've found the strength to forgive, when you've gained wisdom, when you've achieved whatever it is you set out to achieve — you will have developed the courage and fortitude necessary to take on the next challenge that comes your way. You will step out better and stronger than when you went in.

Whatever you may be experiencing during your chrysalis process and however long that process takes, journaling is a helpful tool to assist you in working through your thoughts. Your journal can be symbolic of your chrysalis. It can be the safe place you (as the fully-grown caterpillar secure in her voice and identity) can be free to break down, to melt, to feel, to understand, to rebuild and renew. The truth is, we go in and out of chrysalis moments, because there will always be challenges and opportunities for growth placed before us. Journaling is a wonderful technique to help you do the work. It's effective. It not only allows you to feel the emotions, but also to see and read them. You are documenting your experience every step of the way. And that makes it more valid, more real and more productive. You are saying yes to the journey ahead and playing an active role in your evolution. And when you emerge, you are enlightened and empowered.

In fall of 2015, I hesitantly entered a chrysalis phase, one that I had been putting off for years. I made the decision to return to Vallejo, California, the place where my innocence was taken. It was a step in my journey that had haunted me for years. And after much resistance, I accepted that it was a necessary step if I wanted to grow my courage and believe in my own wings.

After I booked my flight, I began a new journal. My plan was to journal for 30 days leading up to my departure. I did not take my decision to return to California lightly, and I knew that the days leading up to the trip would be a cascade of emotions…a breaking down. I knew I needed to enter this dark place, process the thoughts and develop the courage necessary to face all that my upcoming journey would bring.

I knew I needed to be transformed. And on October 19, 2015, I began a courage-building process that would take me from confusion, anguish and heartbreak to discovery, acceptance and forgiveness. I was ready to do the work, knowing my dark place would become brighter and growth would be achieved.

We have all experienced situations that have initiated a chrysalis process within us. Issues like abuse, bullying, failed friendships and relationships, peer pressure, family difficulties, body image or fear of trying something new…just to name a few. What dark places have you experienced?

_____

_____

_____

_____

_____

_____

_____

_____

_____

_____

_____

_____

_____

_____

_____

What did you learn about yourself during that time?

_____

_____

_____

_____

_____

_____

_____

_____

Was your courage strengthened?

_____

_____

_____

_____

_____

_____

_____

_____

Did you journal during that time? If yes, how did it help? If no, will you consider journaling next time?

_____

_____

_____

_____

_____

_____

_____

_____

The Call of the Chrysalis

I heard my name whispered

I didn't know what to say

I didn't want to hear it

Just wished it would go away

I heard the darkness calling

And I plugged up both my ears

I don't want to grow my courage

Don't want to face my fears

I heard the chrysalis saying

It's not just about my heart

There are others out there waiting

For the wisdom I must impart

So I took the strongest stance I could muster

To provide stability

And I entered the place of darkness

To fight for you and me

I waged war against the dragon

Who blew fire with hate-filled rage

And I documented every step of my quest

Wrote every word upon the page

And with every failed attack in the shadows

The dragon lost his ability to fight

I harnessed his fire and declared it my own

119

And transformed it into light

When the light cracked open my darkened shell

I heard sounds like an angel sings

Amazed by the new thing standing before them

My chrysalis had given me wings

CHAPTER 10

THE HERO'S JOURNEY

Do you believe in heroes? I don't mean like in the movies. I mean everyday people, surviving circumstances designed to destroy them while also providing protection and direction for others. Do you believe in the hero's journey? The quest that the hero reluctantly embarks upon, and, after facing a host of tests and trials, returns from triumphant and valiant? I do. But more importantly, I believe that I am a hero, and so are YOU.

We are the heroes of our own stories. And we are each called to take our hero's journey. The hero's journey is a chrysalis experience. It's the matriarch of all chrysalis moments — a chrysalis process on steroids. It's a defining moment in your story you won't soon forget. And like all chrysalis situations, it takes a measure of courage to embark upon this journey, to trust the process must take place, and to be confident that you will be delivered to the other side...courageous, wiser and brighter.

There are no set-in-stone rules regarding how frequently a hero's journey can occur in one's life. You may embark upon one hero's journey or several. Or perhaps you feel as you've

121

been on the same hero's journey for years. All that matters is you realize that you are the hero; this is your story, and it will be the culmination of your voice, courage and power that writes the ending. Although there are no strict guidelines for this "queen of chrysalis moments," according to American scholar Joseph Campbell, there are 12 common elements that typically present themselves in every hero's journey.

1. Ordinary World: The ordinary world is that not-so comfortable "comfort zone" I warned you about. This is where life is presenting you with a situation that is producing anxiety and fear.

2. Call to Adventure: As the stress is brewing in your ordinary world, things take a turn for the worse, and you receive the call to action…the call to do something big to change the direction of your narrative.

3. Refusal of the Call: Although you know it's time for great change and transformation to begin, your fears feel too powerful. Because of the presence of the unknown and the absence of clarity, you ignore what must be done and refuse to answer this calling.

4. Meeting with the Mentor: After you accept the adventure to which you've been called, a mentor (or

several) shows up. This person or persons will be responsible for providing guidance for the journey ahead. By reading the content of this book and taking part in its reflections, you are allowing me to be one of your mentors — an honor I don't take lightly.

5. Crossing the Threshold: The hero sets out on her journey. She leaves the ordinary world behind and enters the unknown realm — a place of uncertainty.

6. Tests, Allies and Enemies: Test and trials present themselves during this stage. The hero must decide who is friend or foe…who's a part of her squad or a hater. This sequence of smaller battles and tests are preparation for the large one. This can almost be seen as a series of mini chrysalis moments within this larger chrysalis experience.

7. The Approach: During this stage, the final preparation occurs for the mission ahead. The moment of truth is near, and the hero is well-equipped for her fight.

8. The Ordeal: Here, the hero comes face-to-face with her biggest fear. There is a dragon to slay; a beast to tame; a wisdom to be gained; a magical elixir of courage to possess. This is the fight to obtain the treasure she came to win.

9. The Reward: The hero wins her battle and receives the gem she came to find.

10. The Road Back: This is where the hero begins her return home, but she realizes there will be more tests on her journey back. Sometimes, the decision to return home is more difficult to make than the one to leave.

11. The Resurrection: Just as the hero is about to return with her newfound power and knowledge, a final test presents itself, making it all the more important to survive and return.

12. Return with the Elixir: Here, the hero is victorious. You are victorious. You return with *BELIEF*…a deep knowledge of self, intense courage and harnessed personal power. Not only are you prepared to unleash that belief out into the world, but also encourage others to tap into their own.

There's something inexplicable about the hero's journey…that feeling of being pulled down by the darkness yet rising up triumphant.

At times, I feel as though I've been on a hero's journey most of my life. The things I had to face as a five year old were horrific and scary. I was just a little girl…a baby. And when I look back on that time, it's like looking at a different person. That little girl was my hero. She saved me. She survived so I could be here communicating with you today. She survived so I could share our story with you. She survived so that I could return the favor and one day save her. That day has come.

And though I sometimes feel I've been on a never-ending heroic quest, I really wasn't. What I've experienced all these years were small chrysalis moments designed to prepare me for my biggest adventure. They were foreshadowing clues of the adult warrior to come — the hero I would be. The hero that would return and save that little girl...the five-year-old me.

Answering the call was the hardest part. When tension in my life would boil over, the call to the journey would come, and I would ignore it...every time. It was hard to ask questions and investigate a topic that I had been conditioned to conceal. It was difficult to talk to my parents about this. In fact, they remain the hardest ones with whom to discuss this. My body would tense each time I mentioned it to them. I felt I was doing something wrong. My cooperation in the silence protected them from the pain of facing the reality — the reality that their daughter was violated in the home of someone they thought they could trust. As my parents, that hurt them. Every time I broke that silence, every time I addressed it, I felt I was inviting that pain into their lives. But answering the call to this journey didn't just mean inviting pain into their lives. It also meant ushering it into my own. Because my cooperation in the silence also helped me avoid the fact that I felt betrayed by my parents in the aftermath, for avoiding the topic and leaving me to handle it on my own. Sexual abuse is a complex situation. And for years, I wasn't ready for that. I wasn't ready to face my anger towards my abuser, my disappointment in my own mom and dad, or my brokenness inside. But in October of 2015, after a couple of decades of snubbing it, I finally answered. I said yes to the call, and I booked a flight to Vallejo, California.

A trip like this takes more than just arranging a few travel plans. I needed to prepare my heart…to remind myself of my voice and affirm my courage. I had to prepare a place within me to house the personal power that would be realized and harnessed once my adventure was done. You see when you're in the chrysalis…when you're on a hero's journey…you're on the battlefield, and fighting needs to be done. So, I equipped myself with heavy artillery—my journal, wise friends and the word of God.

I want to share one of my journal entries with you. It reads:

"October 27, 2015

22 days until my trip

November…Usually when I think of November, I think of pomegranates, apples, falling leaves and the colors of autumn. It feels good.

November is upon us. It will be here in a few short days, and all I can feel is anxiety. Each time the word November is uttered or if I think of it, my chest tightens. Once November arrives, I will be that much closer. That much closer to returning to the place where innocence was lost. That much closer to returning to the land where the child in me died, leaving but a broken version of youth. The thought of that petrifies me. And so, that is why November may never look, smell or feel the same.

I spoke with [my mother-in-law] at length this evening. She's happy I'm going to Vallejo. She's glad I'll be able to get answers and hopefully be able to close this chapter. But can you ever really close a chapter like this? Can you ever just put something so profound behind you?

Her support means a lot. And it's nice to be able to talk to her…

While talking to her, I expressed my desire to see my abuser, his mother and his brother. I want to come face-to-face with them. I want to see if they remember me and see the looks on their faces as they recall little Donloyn and compare her to the woman before them. Then I listened to Mariah Carey's 'I Wish You Well.' And I had the answer to another question I posed a few days back. The question was, 'What will I say to him…what will I say to my abuser?' I would say, 'Hello, D___ Smith. Do you know who I am? I am Donloyn…all grown up…I'm not five anymore. Have I crossed your mind over the years? Have you thought of me often? Or did you just bury me in the past? I don't hate you. I don't mean you any harm. I just want to look in your face…that same face that used to intimidate me. And I want to say, you did not break me; you did not kill me. If you have not thought of me over the years, I'm certain you will from this point forward. Examine Proverbs 19:29, 1 John 4:4, Philippians 4:9, and Psalm 129:2. And despite what you may think, I wish you well.'"

I share that particular entry with you to illustrate how the combined use of guidance from a trusted friend, journal writing and bible scriptures can help you sort through your emotions and prepare for the battle ahead. As my journey progressed, my journal entries were a roller coaster of emotions, questions and answers. As I went along, some things became clearer. Some things even became more upsetting and more devastating than I had realized. Allowing myself the freedom and space to finally work through my circumstances opened the door to thoughts and feelings I didn't realize I had.

Looking back on it all, my journey possessed every stage of the classic hero's journey. I was plagued in my ordinary world by unresolved pain and feelings of rejection and inadequacy. The call to embark upon my personal journey — that voice within — screamed out to me, time and time again. But I refused to answer. I refused, until I couldn't refuse any longer. Several mentors came forward. Some held my hands the entire way; some at certain times along the journey. But they all imparted wisdom, guidance, love and encouragement. Once I crossed the threshold and returned to Vallejo, there were many tests before me. Allies presented themselves. Old school records, hospital reports and court documents were placed in my hands because of these allies.

My approach and ordeal were the culmination of many events over the course of several days. But one profound thing stands out most...I visited my old house and the old Smith home, not once, but twice. And both times, I just stood there, on the sidewalk, staring. Staring and thinking. Taking it all in.

November 18, 2015

Day One in Vallejo, California

...Then we went to my old neighborhood. We went to a little house on Loyola Way. Everything looked so different. The

little playhouse in the backyard was no longer there. We took pictures.

Then we went around the corner to a house on Pomona Drive…The old Smith house. As soon as we pulled onto the street, my insides began to shake. I felt the anxiety in my chest. And there it was. It has been remodeled just a tad…faux stone work placed on the front and fresh paint, but still the same. I wonder what it looks like on the inside.

When I look at this tiny, eleven-hundred square foot structure, I wonder how anyone could pretend to not know what was going on in the back room. Mrs. Smith knew. She always knew…

November 21st

Last full day in Vallejo

…We went by my old house and the Smith's old house once more. I just needed to breathe it in. [I needed to breathe in] the place I lived with my parents and brother so innocently. [I needed to breathe in] the place where that innocence was snatched, feasted upon and destroyed. My innocence died in that house. I wonder if it somehow lives on, trapped inside of the walls of that 1100sqft structure, crying, dying, begging

to be released and returned to me…me, its rightful owner.
Maybe that sounds ridiculous, but that's how it feels to me…

During my trip to Vallejo, I conquered so much fear. And gained so much strength. And although I was never able to come face-to-face with my violator, I still gained my reward. I was successful in capturing the secret elixir. I had cultivated a deep courage within myself and harnessed my power. And there was no way I would ever lose it or give it away again.

The trip home was difficult. I had no idea it would be. As much as I had accomplished thus far, I knew there was much left to be done. I had to face my parents…share my thoughts and feelings despite the lump in my throat. Share my emotions and all I learned on my trip regardless of the discomfort it brought. That was a difficult thing to do. But I knew I had to see this journey to the end. My voice, my courage, my power and, ultimately, my belief depended on it. My relationships depended on it. My words to you here depended on it.

And I did just that.

Do you believe you are a hero? Share why or why not.

_____

_____

_____

_____

_____

_____

_____

_____

Have you ever received the call? Have you ever heard that small voice within calling you to battle, calling you to come face-to-face with a fear? Did you answer? Or did you ignore it?

_____

_____

_____

_____

_____

_____

_____

_____

_____

_____

_____

_____

_____

Have you ever been on a hero's journey? How did you feel upon the completion of that experience? What did you learn about yourself?

_____

_____

_____

_____

_____

_____

_____

_____

_____

_____

_____

_____

In regards to mentors and trusted friends…what qualities should you look for in a confidant that would deem them qualified to give you guidance prior to or during your personal journey?

_____

_____

_____

_____

_____

_____

_____

_____

Do you have any favorite quotes, inspirations or holy verses that you would take with you on your hero's journey?

_____

_____

_____

_____

_____

_____

_____

_____

Is there a situation going on in your life right now that may eventually result in a hero's journey? Is there a problem in your life that could have a damaging impact on your future self?

_____

_____

_____

_____

_____

_____

_____

_____

_____

_____

_____

_____

_____

_____

_____

_____

_____

_____

Wisteria in Bloom

Sitting at the water's edge
Stillness, glass-like reflection
I recognize her sitting there
Self-assured, yet plagued with gloom

Ignoring echoes in the air
Denial, refusal, rejection
Hands cupped over ears
Serenaded by a dreadful tune

Receiving counsel in her ear
Wisdom, truth and connection
Heart guarded, mind aware
Forewarned of impending doom

Mounting her horse for the journey ahead
Artillery for protection
Shield of Faith and Sword of the Spirit
Words shoot like arrows from her plume

Entering the unknown realm
With an altered sense of direction
Who speaks truth, who speaks lies?
She approaches the darkened tomb

Drawing out her mighty sword
Plunging it deep into the infection
Regaining and reclaiming all that was hers
As the beast falls with a thunderous boom

Returning to the ones she loves
Deep adoration and affection
After a cold, harsh winter of warring
Springtime will be coming soon

Approaching the city early morn
Spring flowers bow in subjection
An assemblage of wisteria clothed in purple
The smells of sweet perfume

Shining brightly with newfound power
Her victory restored perfection
Our hero curtsies gracefully
To the Wisteria in Bloom

STAGE III

POWER

THE BUTTERFLY

CHAPTER 11

<u>PERSONAL POWER</u>

When you enter the chrysalis, you enter as a fully-grown caterpillar. You are prepared for the journey ahead because you have done the work of feeding your voice and developing your identity. But, in order to flourish — in order to transform — you must develop courage. As illustrated, courage is developed when tests, trials and battles are overcome in the dark places. But there's more. A beautiful chain reaction occurs when this courage is developed. As voice and courage collide within the chrysalis, power is harnessed. And not just any power...YOUR power...personal power. That is your reward. That is your magical elixir.

Personal power is an energy. It belongs to you and you alone. Like matter, it can neither be created nor destroyed. It has always and will always exist within you. No one can steal or take it from you.

Remember the buzzing I warned you about? The chaos? The noise? The wasps? That buzzing doesn't just go away because you are no longer a caterpillar. Wasps not only eat caterpillars but also prey on butterflies. And just as the butterfly must be aware of the dangers the wasps present, you, too, must be aware of those who will attempt to steal your power. But, wait. Didn't you just read that no one can steal your power? Yes, that is exactly what you read, and it's true. No one can steal your power, but they can trick you into giving it away.

Personal power is a precious commodity. More priceless than diamonds or gold. Everyone is after it. The problem is that most people don't realize they already possess this exquisite gem. So, instead of going within, to their own personal mines, they'd rather steal the treasure that you've collected from yours. They know that stripping you of your power is a death sentence. They think if they can kill your spirit and feast upon your strength, they can claim your power for their own. Clipping your wings, grounding you, preventing you from soaring to new heights…that's what makes them feel superior to you.

So, how do these "wasps" go about stealing your personal power? Through selfishness, jealousy, ego and pride. These characteristics, which manifest from unresolved self-doubt and fear, are typical of wasps. They never did the work of feeding their identities or developing their voices. They don't know or understand who they are. They have a threatened sense of self and have never done the preparation necessary to enter into a chrysalis experience where fear could be overcome and courage developed.

Who are these wasps? They are the bullies. The mean girls. The ones who ridicule you for being different, unique and original. The ones who smile in your face, yet secretly condemn you to others. The ones who hurt and reject you, time and again. The list goes on. These are the individuals who want you to stay in tiny, ever-shrinking boxes. The ones who are threatened by your growth and potential. They are threatened by yours because they cannot see their own. Your strength is intimidating. And the only thing the wasps know how to do is attack that which they view as a threat.

Are you powerless against the attacks? Absolutely not. Your voice, courage and personal power are all you need to combat these vicious attacks. Remember, remain true to the need to be heard versus that longing to belong. Continue to be your strong, unique, spectacular self. Continue to raise your voice…make a positive impact. Continue to encourage others by sharing your light—the light that you discovered after having traveled through the darkened places. Your light will shine as a beacon of hope for others like you. Your voice will sound as a trumpet and will call out to beautiful, bright souls from all around. Keep your talents and gifting aimed on your purpose…the collective purpose we all share, which is to affect positive change in the lives of others. By courageously standing firm in your identity, you demonstrate your unwillingness to surrender your personal power. You are a force, and your greatness will be seen.

You will have moments when you doubt your power. Moments when you lose all hope in your greatness. That's normal. It's okay. We all have moments of weakness…times when we can't hold the fear at bay. Sometimes we feel tired and ready to just give up. Don't. Don't ever give up. Feel weak for a moment if you must. But do not stay there long. Remind yourself of your power…the identity and courage that it spawned from. Remind yourself of your victories, all the battles you fought and won. Talk with a mentor. Journal. Read scriptures and inspirational quotes. Do whatever you have to do, just don't quit.

I understand how it feels to have your power threatened. I understand how it feels to be tricked into giving it away. Being molested and raped; being rejected because of my racial and cultural makeup; being shunned because my different experiences; being told I wasn't good at anything and convinced that I had no talent…All of those situations were designed to strip me of my power…to convince me that I was powerless and incapable of great things. But you are a warrior. You are a hero. When you find yourself in that position, remember you possess the artillery. Not only are you are fully-equipped with the same weapons you had in the chrysalis, but also you have emerged with a renewed sense of self, unshakable bravery and unstoppable power. And those three components, when used properly, can obliterate any attack against you.

Earlier this year, I had a moment of powerlessness. The following is a journal entry expressing those feelings of hopelessness and defeat:

February 21, 2016

…Boundaries is a foreign concept, obviously. And personal power…it is clear I have none. So, how can I write a book for teens encouraging their voice, courage and power when I have flopped in all three areas? I'm trying so hard to be a peacemaker, to be positive, to be better…when all I really want is to be left alone. Their noise is drowning me out, pulling me under and suffocating me. I am slowly dying…

Yes, I had a "feel-sorry-for-myself, woe-is-me" moment. But I quickly got back on track. I did not allow that moment of expressing frustration take over. That moment's only purpose was to serve as a release…an opportunity to exhale the toxicity and make room to inhale what's good. You are allowed those moments, but you cannot stay there. Otherwise, all you'll be blowing out is a heap of destructive negativity.

Remember, YOU are powerful. You need not *discover* that fact on your own. You just need to **uncover** it. That is what every self-aware woman in your life should be instilling in you. Your power is precious. It is within you. Once you've uncovered it, guard it with all that you are. Do not guard it with a closed fist, thinking someone can steal it. No, instead, guard it with open hands, an open mind and an open heart. Guard it by reaffirming your identity. Guard it by constantly challenging yourself to show up with courage. Guard it by consistently bringing your brave self to each opportunity. You have greatness in you. And it is your duty to use that greatness to soar to unimaginable heights. In doing so, you will change the world.

Do you believe you possess greatness? Do you know that you are powerful?

_____

_____

_____

_____

_____

_____

_____

_____

What are your greatest strengths?

_____

_____

_____

_____

_____

_____

_____

_____

List the "wasps" in your life. Who or what represents the "buzzing" that surrounds you and threatens your power? Will you give your power away?

_____

_____

_____

_____

_____

_____

_____

_____

How will you use your gifts to change the world?

_____

_____

_____

_____

_____

_____

_____

_____

_____

How will you encourage other girls to uncover and use their greatness?

_____

_____

_____

_____

_____

_____

_____

_____

_____

Who or what inspires you to be great?

_____

_____

_____

_____

_____

_____

_____

_____

When do you feel most powerful?

_____

_____

_____

_____

_____

_____

_____

_____

_____

_____

_____

CHAPTER 12

<u>BREAKING FREE</u>

When the butterfly is fully formed, her chrysalis begins to thin and becomes transparent. It is no longer thick and opaque in color. The new creation housed beneath this almost clear layer is unmistakable. You can see the wings, its unique patterns and deep hues. This phase of the journey is complete, and the butterfly begins to break free from its tiny encasing.

Like the butterfly, when you come to the end of your chrysalis experience, a clearness is attained. Light begins to seep into the once darkened spaces. Walls become thin. And your transformation is apparent. But most importantly, your evolution is evident to you. This is called clarity.

According to Dictionary.com, clarity is defined as a "clearness or lucidity as to perception or understanding; freedom from indistinctness or ambiguity. The state or quality of being clear or transparent to the eye; pellucidity: the clarity of pure water."

In the chrysalis, after courage is developed and personal power is harnessed, clarity comes. A clearness manifests. Lucidity and light penetrate what was once dark. There is no ambiguity. You are free. Free from the paralysis that doubt brings to your life. Freedom from the shadows that fear casts over you. Free not only to step into the light with a clear understanding of your voice, courage and power, but also with the knowledge of how to use them. Clarity strengthens voice, courage and personal power. It smooths the jagged edges of your purpose. Things become more defined. Your vision of yourself and for the future come into focus.

Notice the progression and process of your evolution, thus far. It happens in steps:

1. You roam about collecting information to feed your voice.
2. Once voice is developed, you enter the chrysalis to grow your courage.
3. The union of voice and courage give rise to personal power.
4. After personal power is harnessed, clarity rushes in.
5. Ultimately, power and clarity join forces and you break free.

Welcome to the world! You are now an amazing work of nature...a beautiful butterfly with fully developed wings, capable of reaching incredible heights. But, you can't fly just yet. Please realize, you've been through a lot. In addition to having to learn who you are as a person, you've had to endure the buzzing and the noise of the world; you've been through challenging situations and dark places; you've had your courage tested; you've received answers to your questions and solutions to problems; you've been hit with the realization that you have this awesome power and that you are capable of greatness. That's a lot. You can't jump into full flight mode and expect it to turn out well. You have to be still.

When the butterfly emerges from her chrysalis, she is most vulnerable. She is fragile and must rest next to the chrysalis' remains to allow her wings time to dry. The same is true for you. When you emerge from your chrysalis, you must also allow your newly-formed wings the opportunity to rest, to dry. You must take a moment to catch your breath from the journey you've just completed. It's a chance to process all you've been through and absorb everything you've learned.

My hero's journey was exhausting. Although I came through it more courageous and powerful than ever, I was drained. Spending a month preparing for my trip was an emotional roller coaster all on its own. Actually stepping foot into the city that my family ran from after all those years ago to gather pieces of my unspoken and forgotten story was overwhelming. Dredging up old memories and pain from the past is excruciating. But, sometimes you must wake the giant in order to lay it to rest. After returning from Vallejo, facing my parents was another hurdle to cross. When all was said and done, I was a big sack of conflicting emotion. I was strong and clear in who I had become. I felt victorious, but, at the same time, I was weak. I had my wings, but they were still wet. I had my wings, but I could not fly.

Here are some lines from a journal entry I wrote during my resting period:

December 31, 2015

Today was rather difficult. I'm feeling so many things right now. It's overwhelming. I feel everything, even conflicting emotions at the same time. I feel happiness and sadness; anger and forgiveness; understanding and confusion; and so on. How opposites can co-exist is completely beyond me, but I'm just trusting the process..."

After the caterpillar enters the chrysalis phase, it is broken down into a slurry — a wet biological mass of information that will serve as the building blocks for the butterfly. When it emerges from the chrysalis, residual dampness from its former self is still present on its wings. The same is true for you. Even after you emerge with your marvelous wings, residual thoughts, feelings and emotions will still be present.

Reread the journal entry. Notice I was in a strange state of conflicting emotion — that moment in time when old and new feelings share the same atmosphere just before old thoughts are evicted by the new. Sometimes, old emotions merge with the new, shaping new ideas and possibilities. This is what the drying phase looks like. This is you — the hero, the butterfly, the new creation — resting, taking a breath, processing, feeling, allowing. At this point, all you are required to do is remain still and trust the process. You are vulnerable. You are spent. You've just stepped off the battlefield. And though you are strong and clear in your identity and personal power, this is the time to recover from all you've learned and endured.

Have you experienced this resting phase? Why is it important to be still?

_____

_____

_____

_____

_____

_____

_____

This is when you are most vulnerable. How can you guard yourself from the attacks of your personal wasps?

_____

_____

_____

_____

_____

_____

_____

_____

How does it feel to break free?

_____

_____

_____

_____

_____

_____

_____

_____

CHAPTER 13

<u>THE BELIEF IN WINGS</u>

Once its wings have dried and it has rested, a butterfly doesn't wonder if she can fly. She knows she can. She believes in this gifting of hers although she has never before executed such an amazing power. She knows. She trusts. She is clear in her purpose and her unique abilities. She believes.

What does it mean to believe? As defined by Dictionary.com, to believe means "to have confidence in the truth, existence or reliability of something, although without absolute proof one is right in doing so: Only if one believes in something can one act purposefully." Believing means possessing a knowledge that something, someone or some idea exists even though you have no evidence of it. It's a renewed mindset. It's a mystical, magical, dreamy state of mind that says all good things are possible. It is faith and hope. It is trust.

As you've already learned, when you break free from the chrysalis, the blend of voice, courage and power give way to clarity. As a result, this clearness of mind results in an understanding of purpose and your personal calling. Although they are oftentimes used synonymously, purpose and calling are different. Purpose is what links us all, as we were all created in God's image for one collective purpose — to affect positive change in the lives of others. However, because of our unique abilities and gifts, we are each called to fulfill this purpose in different ways. We each have our own personal calling. You may be called to make a positive difference in the lives of others through the gift of science, mathematics, athletics, dance or music, writing or art. We are all called differently. But, through that calling, we fulfill the same purpose.

When you add clarity and purpose to this beautiful blend of voice, courage and power, you are ready to demonstrate belief. But how do you demonstrate belief? The answer… through action! Belief requires action. It requires doing; it is not passive.

Let's examine the last line in the definition of believe once more: "Only if one believes in something can one act purposefully." You must believe in order to "act purposefully." That is, demonstrating specific action that is rooted in purpose. The butterfly can undergo great transformation, break free from the chrysalis and allow her wings time to dry, but if she never takes purposeful action — if she never actively flutters her wings — she will be forever grounded. If she does not exercise her power, she will never take flight. But, in order to demonstrate her power, she must believe! Action and belief go hand-in-hand. One cannot exist without the other. Faith without works is dead. Belief without action is pointless.

The whole purpose for this process — this process of caterpillar to butterfly, this process of doubt-filled girl to influential young woman — is to harness personal power and develop the clarity necessary to activate that power. It's not enough to have the power. You have to be able to turn that power on. Much like electricity in a home, so too is your personal power. The wiring behind a light switch plate houses the power, but it is useless until we turn the switch to the On position. By flipping the switch, we bring light to the situation. By flipping the switch, we activate the power that already exists. Light is power in action. Your light is your personal power in action.

So how do you take action? Through the use of your wings! Action is displayed by using your wings.

Your wings are designed for greatness. Again…your wings are designed for greatness! Your wings are your gifts, talents, goals and aspirations. They house your dreams and passions for the future. Strength and energy rests upon them; they carry harnessed personal power. As you begin to move them—as your wings begin to flutter—that power is activated. And your inner light is awakened. And that light generated from taking action creates the warmth and confidence necessary to take the next big step, to put your next awesome move into action, and so on.

Power and light are essential to the butterfly. Butterflies are solar-powered. Did you know that? Their wings are covered with tiny scales that act as solar panels. Just as you harness personal power, they harness power from the sun, and they use that light energy to warm their wings for flight. These delicate wings house tremendous strength, capable of taking the butterfly to great heights. Some reports have documented Monarch butterflies flying as high as 11,000 feet!

After my drying phase was complete—once my period of rest and stillness in the aftermath of my trip to Vallejo was done—I had one question. *"What's next, God?"* After developing my voice in the caterpillar stage, I entered my chrysalis prepared—fully expecting to attain courage. To my surprise, not only did I emerge with courage, but also power, clarity and an accurate knowledge of purpose. Now that I was in possession of these exquisite jewels, I knew there was something great I was expected to do with them. But what? And then the answer came...I needed to adorn my wings with them! I needed to polish my gifts, talents, goals and aspirations with my precious gems of voice, courage, power, clarity and purpose. I needed to bring these elements together and *believe* in the brilliance that would result. Bringing them together required action. Bringing them together would create a superpower. When you ignite your superpower with action, you create a magnificent light as your wings lift you to unimaginable heights.

My answer was this book. My action was writing these words for you. I adorned my wings and activated their power to create a light for you.

January 23, 2016

I'm working on my book! The Belief in Wings! A book for young girls to encourage them to believe in the power they already possess. It will be a journey. A journey from voice to courage to power. I want the book to include writing prompts, areas where the girls can share their thoughts, ideas and wisdoms. Initially I was worried, thinking this wasn't the right action to take. I prayed about it and just went with it. Yesterday, [my aunt] died. One week before her birthday. It was a rainy day. Both literally and metaphorically. I couldn't

163

focus. I couldn't write. I was going through some old files and came across a video I recorded and published the day after teaching a writing workshop at a teen empowerment conference. The video recharged my batteries. It reminded me of the purpose of this book. I decided to share it on social media and noticed that I had originally shared it two years ago on January 29th, [my aunt's] birthday! Confirmation from God! This book is definitely the correct action. I am in awe...humbled...ecstatic! Praise Jehovah from whom all blessings flow."

As I shine my light for you, my hope is that you will uncover your power, put it to action and shine your light for others to see. In doing so, we create a chain reaction, a Butterfly Effect. The light, energy and power that radiate from our wings is remarkable. It creates a ripple, a wave of energy capable of stimulating big change. All we must do is believe in the power they hold.

When you believe in your greatness and take specific action with regard to that greatness, you are unleashing your power. You are releasing your strength and energy into the world. You are taking flight. You are demonstrating *The Belief in Wings.*

Describe your wings! What are your gifts, talents, goals and aspirations? What are your dreams and passions for the future?

_____

_____

_____

_____

_____

_____

_____

_____

_____

_____

_____

_____

_____

_____

_____

_____

_____

_____

_____

_____

Do you feel confident in your greatness? Do you doubt your wings, or do you believe in the power they hold?

_____

_____

_____

_____

_____

_____

_____

_____

_____

_____

_____

_____

_____

_____

_____

_____

_____

_____

_____

_____

_____

_____

How will you use your power? What specific action or actions do you plan to take to demonstrate the belief in your wings?

_____

_____

_____

_____

_____

_____

_____

_____

_____

_____

_____

_____

_____

_____

_____

_____

_____

_____

_____

_____

_____

_____

On the Wings of a Butterfly

On the wings of a butterfly
The things I would see
The places I'd go
The people I'd meet

I'd flit and I'd flutter
Without a care in the world
Serenaded by the laughter
Of each boy and girl

Secure in my abilities
With a strong sense of voice
I'd spread hope-filled inspiration
And let my spirit rejoice

The courage in my wings
Would dry the tears from my eyes
From the saddening lows
And the treacherous highs

My delicate frame
Would be powerful indeed
With determination and confidence
I'd know I'd succeed

I'd carry vision for the future
Rooted in purpose and clarity
My calling would be my own
Me, the awesome rarity

I'd absorb and emit
And transfer magnificent light
My wings would be evidence
Of my greatness and might

And at the end of the day
When I dream of grand things
I'd know they're all possible
'Cuz I'd believe in my wings

DONLOYN LEDUFF GADSON

FINAL THOUGHTS

Congratulations! You are a beautiful butterfly destined for magnificent things! But before you fly off to explore the world, there are a few last things you need to know.

Your journey doesn't end here. You've uncovered your power and have gained your wings, but this is just the beginning. Once developed, wings must be nurtured in order to maintain their strength. That means you must continue to push yourself toward greatness. Continue to dream and make bold moves to achieve those dreams. Say yes to opportunities that scare you. In doing so, you keep your courageous spirit vibrant and alive.

You will also experience more tests and trials. Difficulties and hardships are a normal part of life. Again, choose courage. Face these challenges head on, knowing that you possess every good thing you need to win. If you fail to believe in your wings and the precious gems that adorn them, they will lose their strength. Your delicate wings are capable of fluttering to amazing heights; however, if you stop believing in them, they will wilt and wither.

If you move away from your power, you will move back in the direction of self-doubt. As other beautiful butterflies around you continue to believe and achieve great things, your fear of spreading your wings and traveling to unknown places will prevent you from being happy for them. Consequently, the sound of your voice will begin to change. Confidence in your identity will begin to crumble. And you will begin to resemble the bees and wasps. Bitterness will lead you to create the buzzing sounds intended to distract others from developing their identities. That behavior is destructive as it can convince others to abandon their personal power.

These are the things that can happen if you allow fear to direct you. This is what the result will be if you don't use all of the amazing traits that already exist within you. This is what will happen if you don't believe in your greatness. Now that you know who you are and the immense power you possess, you mustn't throw that away.

Let me tell you a little story...

~

Once upon a time in a land not so far away, there was a beautiful valley nestled amidst two hills. There were open meadows filled with Milk Thistle, Shasta Daisies and Purple

Cone Flower. There was a stream...wild flowers lined the sides of its banks.

This beautiful valley was the home to a community of butterflies in a wide array of colors and types. The butterflies flew along the base of the hillside, throughout the meadows and near the stream. However, they never ventured beyond the valley. They never even flew to the top of the hillside to take a peek at what lay beyond this barrier. They were content with what they knew and had no interest in expanding their horizons. The valley was a beautiful place, and they were just fine with that.

But for one butterfly, this was not enough. The valley was beautiful indeed, but she wanted to learn new things, see new places and travel as far as her glorious wings could possibly take her.

Blossom had always been unique. She carried herself with great confidence. Even as a caterpillar, she was secure in her voice. Amazingly, she had even learned to differentiate between the harmless buzzing of the bees and the dangerous buzzing of the wasps — a skill her mother had taught her. When the bees would enter the valley, Blossom would continue eating leaves while all the other caterpillars would scurry for shelter. Even when the wasps would pay an unwelcomed visit, Blossom would boldly lift her caterpillar voice and let out the loudest squeak she could muster. *"Squeak!"* She was the bravest of them all — a trait that pleased her mother greatly.

Sadly, just before Blossom entered her chrysalis, her mother's time had come to an end. She was saddened by the death of her mother. She missed seeing her flutter high and gracefully across the blue skies. She missed seeing her mother fly over the hillside and out of sight. She would wonder where her mother went when she took these grand adventures.

It was the memory of her amazing mother that encouraged Blossom's greatness. So each day after becoming a butterfly, Blossom ventured beyond the valley, taking in new sights and expanding her horizons.

The other butterflies did not like this at all. They scoffed at Blossom's curious spirit and ridiculed her for seeking more.

They began to sound like the bees and wasps. Always buzzing around her, they did everything they could to dissuade Blossom from setting out on her journey each day.

But no matter how hard they tried to convince her that she was behaving foolishly, Blossom continued on her quest to discover amazing things. Each morning, after fluttering about in the valley, Blossom would fly high above the meadows and cross over the hillside.

She saw mountains, rivers and the ocean. She saw happy children playing in parks, far more than the few who would occasionally visit the valley to play. She visited the bushes and flower gardens of homes in quiet neighborhoods and frequented city parks surrounded by large buildings and honking horns.

And each day, when Blossom would return to her home in the valley, the other butterflies would laugh, point and stare. Some would whisper, while others would jeer.

One day upon returning from an exciting adventure, the taunting from the others was far worse than it had ever been. And Blossom had had enough.

"I don't understand. Why are all of you always so mean and spiteful?" said Blossom to the others. "Why do you poke fun at me every day, and why is today worse than all the others?"

Bianca, who always seemed to be at the center of the mockery, fluttered forward.

"Blossom, just look at yourself," she said with a disgusted smirk. "You leave this valley every day, stretch your wings beyond their limits and spread them far and wide. And each day when you return, your wings are larger and grander than the day before. Now look at you! You are monstrous and hideously huge — a disgrace amongst butterflies."

Blossom looked around at them all. She knew the way they saw her was all wrong. Dropping her head at the sadness of this situation, she drew in a deep breath and calmly responded.

"Bianca, this is just not true. Perhaps, it is all of you who should look at yourselves."

They all looked around at one another, puzzled at the point Blossom was trying to make.

"Have you all not noticed how much higher you have to fly before you get to the delicious bud of the Milk Thistle?"

A few eyes began to open and expressions began to change. They hadn't thought about it before, but now that Blossom mentioned it, they realized that was true. They quickly shook off any effect this truth had had upon them, and continued to scowl at Blossom.

Blossom went on.

"And have you all not noticed how long it takes you to flutter from one side of the stream to the other?"

Again, their expressions began to change.

"And what about how large the Purple Cone Flower is when you rest upon it, or how you must steady yourself when drinking from the Shasta daisies so you don't become stuck in its center or buried beneath its petals?"

By this time, everyone was nodding in agreement. Blossom was correct…these things were true. But until this very moment, it had never occurred to any of them.

Blossom looked around at them all and said, "The flowers in the meadow have not changed. The hillside has not grown, and the stream has not widened." She flew towards a Shasta daisy and landed upon it. "Notice my size compared to this flower. I'm quite normal."

Everyone looked confused. Blossom did appear to be normal in size next to the daisy. They all looked at one another and then back at Blossom.

"I love adventure! Broadening my horizons and spreading my wings has not caused me to become hideously huge," she said.

"Well then what is going on here, Blossom," said Bianca in a flustered panic.

"Don't you see?" responded Blossom. "It is not me and my wings that have become grand and monstrous. It is you and your wings that have become withered and wilted."

~

In the story, Blossom possesses every precious trait necessary to have confidence in her greatness, and she adorns her wings with them. She is secure in her voice and demonstrates courage daily. She knows how to access the harnessed power within and is excited to take action daily to achieve her dreams. She believes in the strength and gifting of her wings.

No matter the obstacles you face, never doubt the power that dwells within you. Never doubt your strength and gifting. Doubt can be so convincing when it tells you you're not worthy. But, you were designed for greatness. Feed your voice with inspiration and view each hardship as an opportunity to grow your courage. As you begin to evolve from a place of self-doubt to personal power, you will become a force capable of reaching amazing heights.

Butterfly, you were made to fly. All you have to do is believe…Believe in your wings!

www.ingramcontent.com/pod-product-compliance
Lightning Source LLC
Chambersburg PA
CBHW070404090426
42733CB00009B/1525